More Praise for *After the Taliban*

"*After the Taliban* is a superb read. U.S. Special Envoy to Afghanistan James Dobbins was masterful in orchestrating the peace following decades of violence and war. He stood up their nation's fragile participatory government. Those of us on the ground in Afghanistan during the difficult days of 2001 so admired the skill with which he represented America. This book will be a primer in the study of diplomacy for decades to come."
—GARY BERNTSEN, FORMER CIA OFFICER AND AUTHOR OF *JAWBREAKER: THE ATTACK ON BIN LADEN AND AL QAEDA*

"Ambassador Dobbins probably knows better than anyone else the strengths and weaknesses of the American approach to what they call *"nation building"* and this knowledge is perfectly well illustrated in the case of Afghanistan in the aftermath of 9/11. His is an insider's account of the successful diplomacy leading to the formation of the Karzai government, but he also highlights the lack of follow-through from the United States, the international community as a whole, and the Afghan authorities that left the field open for a resurgent Taliban."
—LAKHDAR BRAHIMI, FORMER SPECIAL REPRESENTATIVE OF THE UN SECRETARY GENERAL FOR AFGHANISTAN

"This compact and lively book provides the first direct, firsthand account of the rebuilding of post–9/11 Afghanistan. From Bagram air base in Afghanistan to the Petersberg guest house outside Bonn, by way of the corridors of power in Washington, Dobbins shows how skillful diplomacy and cooperation can lay the foundations of recovery from protracted war. He also shows how the Bush administration's ideological and doctrinal blinders inspired a series of decisions that nearly undermined the initial successes in Afghanistan—decisions that have had to be undone, one by one, and usually far too late."
—BARNETT RUBIN, SENIOR FELLOW, NEW YORK UNIVERSITY'S CENTER ON INTERNATIONAL COOPERATION, AND AUTHOR OF *THE FRAGMENTATION OF AFGHANISTAN*

AFTER THE TALIBAN

AFTER THE TALIBAN

Nation-Building in Afghanistan

JAMES F. DOBBINS

POTOMAC BOOKS, INC.
WASHINGTON, D.C.

Library of Congress Cataloging-in-Publication Data

Dobbins, James, 1942–
After the Taliban : nation-building in Afghanistan / James F. Dobbins. — 1st ed.
   p. cm.
Includes index.
ISBN 978-1-59797-083-9 (hardcover : alk. paper)
1. Afghanistan—History—2001- 2. United States—Foreign relations—Afghanistan. 3. Afghanistan—Foreign relations—United States. 4. Nation-building—Afghanistan. I. Title.
DS371.4.D63 2008
958.104'7—dc22

                                                        2008017401

Printed in the United States of America on acid-free paper that meets the American National Standards Institute Z39-48 Standard.

Potomac Books, Inc.
22841 Quicksilver Drive
Dulles, Virginia 20166

First Edition

10 9 8 7 6 5 4 3 2 1

CONTENTS

PREFACE

THE AFGHAN CAMPAIGN OF 2001 HAS BEEN COVERED from several perspectives. Gen. Tommy Franks, who commanded U.S. military forces, treated the period in his autobiography, *American Soldier*. Gary Schroen and Gary Berntsen, who led two of the Central Intelligence Agency (CIA) paramilitary teams that preceded the American forces into Afghanistan, told their stories in *First In: An Insider's Account of How the CIA Spearheaded the War on Terror in Afghanistan* and *Jawbreaker: The Attack on bin Laden and al-Qaeda—a Personal Account by the CIA's Key Field Commander* (with Ralph Pezzullo), respectively. This work is intended to provide a similarly personal account of American diplomacy during this period.

I would like to thank my many colleagues at the RAND Corporation for all the advice, encouragement, and support they have provided. Several members of my negotiating team contributed their own recollections of our travels together in late 2001. Col. Jack Gill, my military adviser during that period, provided an invaluable chronology of our mission and recalled several evocative moments. Craig Karp provided a photographic record. Lakhdar Brahimi, the top United Nations (UN) official dealing with Afghanistan, and former Afghan foreign minister Abdullah Abdullah both helped refine my account of the events in which we all participated. Barnett Rubin, our country's foremost expert on Afghanistan and another participant in the diplomacy of late 2001, was good enough to go over an early version of my manuscript and suggested many corrections, additions, and interpretations. Joy Merck help-ed correct and format more versions of this work than she or I care to recall.

From a personal standpoint, the assignment I received in October 2001 to represent the United States to the Afghan opposition—the opportunity to head a major negotiation with broad authority and minimal guidance, backed by the full panoply of national power and buttressed by unified international support—would have been any diplomat's dream. Success attended these efforts with almost unbelievable speed. Within a few short weeks, the Taliban had been routed and a moderate, broadly based, and representative government installed in its place.

Unfortunately, this deceptively easy initial success in Afghanistan emboldened American policymakers. Before Afghanistan's reconstruction had even begun, the Bush administration's attention shifted to the next campaign in its "global war on terror." By early 2002, the pattern had been set for Afghanistan's reconstruction. Rhetorically, President George W. Bush would hail that effort as a new Marshall Plan. Practically, it would be the most poorly resourced American venture into nation-building in more than sixty years.

Now, more than six years later, the war in Afghanistan has become more intense. Most experts believe its successful resolution is at best five to ten years off. This story is of that early triumph, those missed opportunities, and the flawed decisions that continue to shape the current Afghan conflict.

1

FIRST CONTACT

WE BOARDED OUR FLIGHT FROM TASHKENT, Uzbekistan, in the early morning. The plane was a white, unadorned Lockheed L-100, with civilian markings. It belonged to a small fleet of anonymous transports that had been flying Central Intelligence Agency (CIA) agents, arms, and equipment to the Afghan resistance for the past several weeks.

We sat in bucket seats that lined each side of the fuselage. Pieces of equipment and crates of supplies were secured to the floor between us. My party included representatives of the secretary of defense, the chairman of the Joint Chiefs of Staff (JCS), and the CIA director. We composed the first American diplomatic mission to enter Afghanistan in more than twelve years.

Accompanying us was a small group of Afghans, led by a medical doctor whom I had met for the first time the previous day. Dr. Abdullah Abdullah was a comparatively young man, perhaps forty years old. He was a protégé of Ahmed Shah Massoud, the charismatic military leader of the Afghan resistance, and he had served as its primary liaison with the outside world. Al Qaeda agents had assassinated Massoud several weeks earlier, just two days before their attacks on the World Trade Center and the Pentagon.

As we waited on the tarmac for takeoff, an Uzbek customs official sporting enormous, saucer-shaped, Soviet-era military headgear came on board to stamp our passports. Clandestine or not, our group had to observe local border formalities.

Once our aircraft had reached cruising altitude the pilot invited Abdullah and me to join him on the flight deck, where we had a stunning view of the mountain ranges below and could enjoy greater privacy than the main cabin afforded. Here we were also better insulated against the engine noise. For the next two hours we held our first private conversation.

Dr. Abdullah was in a delicate position. He represented a regime that, until a few days earlier, had been little more than a government in exile. Since its ouster from the capital of Kabul in 1996, the Northern Alliance had controlled a steadily diminishing sliver of Afghan territory. For the past couple of years its troops had operated out of mountainous strongholds along the borders with Tajikistan and Uzbekistan, using arms and money the governments of Russia, Iran, and India supplied, and had challenged the Taliban regime in Kabul. Along with the Taliban's own record of abuse and misgovernment, the Northern Alliance's efforts had been sufficient to deny that regime international legitimacy, but the Northern Alliance had posed no real threat to the Taliban's hold on the country.

The power balance in Afghanistan began to change rather dramatically in the weeks following al Qaeda's attacks on New York and Washington on September 11, 2001. By early November, Northern Alliance forces, their combat effectiveness greatly enhanced by American airpower, had routed Taliban formations guarding the provincial capital of Mazar-e-Sharif. Three days later the Northern Alliance had breached the capital's last defenses and marched into Kabul.

Less than a week after Kabul's fall, Dr. Abdullah and I were on our way to Afghanistan to meet with his government's political and military leadership. My mission was to persuade him and his colleagues, who were just beginning to reoccupy the ministries, barracks, palaces, and personal homes from which they had been evicted five years earlier, to dissolve their administration and join other Taliban opponents in a more broadly based government. The other leaders Washington had in mind were mostly émigrés who had fled Afghanistan during the past thirty years. The most distinguished of these men was the former king, Mohammed Zahir Shah, who had been driven into exile in 1973. At this point I could only imagine what the Northern Alliance leadership, having spent years fighting and dying, or, at least, living in considerable discomfort in the Afghan mountains, would think of our proposal.

2

As the sun rose in the sky and glittered off the snow-capped mountains below us, Abdullah spoke with controlled passion of the travails his country had experienced. He expressed particular bitterness about Pakistan's role in promoting the rise of a fundamentalist, radically anti-Western regime in Kabul. Pakistan's purpose in fostering the Taliban, Abdullah explained, had been to create a reservoir of expertise and trained manpower from which it could draw in mounting its own campaign of bombings, assassinations, and terrorist attacks designed to break the Indian government's hold on the disputed province of Kashmir.

Abdullah also spoke critically of American policy in the decade that had followed the Soviets' 1989 withdrawal from Afghanistan. The United States had resolutely turned its back on his country, which American covert efforts had helped free from Soviet occupation. He described his own most recent meetings with American officials who represented the administration of George W. Bush. Their only interest, he said, had been in recovering Stinger shoulder-launched, antiaircraft missiles the United States had supplied to the anti-Soviet mujahideen in the late 1980s.

Eventually, Abdullah shifted to the issue before us. His colleagues in the Northern Alliance leadership knew Washington wanted them to join in constituting a more broadly based successor to the Taliban regime. Some understood the need for this step. Others needed convincing. One obstacle was Burhanuddin Rabbani, a conservative cleric of Tajik ethnicity who had been inaugurated president of Afghanistan in 1992 and maintained his claim to that office ever since. Having just moved back into the presidential palace in Kabul, Rabbani was understandably loath to leave. My most difficult task, Abdullah warned, would be persuading him that doing so was necessary.

Abdullah said some of his colleagues wanted to broaden the base of their current government, which was comprised largely of Tajik, Uzbek, and Hazara leaders from the north, center, and west of the county, to include greater representation from the predominantly Pashtun south and east. Abdullah then went further than I had expected, stating that Afghanistan's next leader should be a Pashtun and should come from outside the Northern Alliance.

Was he suggesting, I asked, that the former king, Zahir Shah, return to assume this role? I knew that Zahir was widely respected throughout the country. Many in Afghanistan regarded his reign, from 1933 to his exile in 1973, as a golden age, especially compared with all that had followed. Now eighty-seven years old, this venerable figure had lived the subsequent decades in a comfortable villa on the outskirts of Rome, and I had visited him there a week earlier. Many in Washington felt that Zahir might act as a unifying figure among the Afghan populace, enjoying support not only in the Pashtun south, whence the royal family originated, but throughout the country. It occurred to me that Abdullah might be proposing that the former king, given his age and personality, should resume a largely symbolic role and leave effective power with the current Northern Alliance leadership.

Abdullah surprised me further, insisting that Afghanistan's next leader needed to be young and vigorous enough to actually lead the country and run the government. Abdullah acknowledged the people generally respected the former king; however, Zahir had never been a particularly decisive figure. Moreover, whatever executive capacity he may once have possessed had now diminished with age. This impression tallied with the one I had formed during my own visit with the former king.

"We need more than a figurehead," Abdullah insisted. "We need someone who will be able to deal with the terrible challenges Afghanistan now faces."

"Did you have anyone in mind?" I inquired.

"Hamid Karzai would be an acceptable choice," Abdullah suggested.

This suggestion was promising. Only a few days earlier the head of Pakistan's main intelligence service, whose organization had sponsored and supported the Taliban for nearly a decade, had also suggested Karzai to me as a leader who would likely be acceptable both to Pakistan and to Pashtun-dominated southern Afghanistan. Now Pakistan's most vocal critic had put forth the same candidate.

How broadly, I asked, did his colleagues in the Northern Alliance leadership share these views? Opinion was divided, Abdullah responded. Several who were closest to the deceased Ahmed Shah Massoud, including Interior Minister Younis Qanooni and Defense Minister Mohammed Fahim, agreed with Abdullah. He thought others could be persuaded, although it would take time.

SOON AFTER we crossed into Afghanistan, the mountains below us gave way to a vast, dusty, dun-colored plain devoid of water, vegetation, or any sign of life. We saw many large, sprawling complexes filled with mud-covered structures surrounded by palisaded walls but no color or movement. They appeared to be the remains of some lost civilization and as lifeless as the pre-Columbian Hopi villages of the American Southwest. These complexes were not the prehistoric remnants of a long dead people but the blasted products of a raging conflict. Two decades of civil war had turned this once irrigated, fertile, and populous region into a desert.

Our destination was Bagram, a Soviet-era airfield some twenty miles north of Kabul. This sprawling base once served as the hub for Soviet military operations throughout the country. Afterward, it had lain in the no-man's-land between Northern Alliance forces holed up in the surrounding mountains and the Taliban, which controlled the southern lowlands stretching out toward Kabul. On this terrain a week earlier Taliban forces had sought to make their last stand short of the capital, and American airpower crushed them.

Other than a large expanse of cracked and crumbling tarmac, little was left of what had once been a major military base. The few remaining structures were all badly damaged. To one side stood an apparently uninhabited control tower. We saw no sign of ground crews, hangars, terminals, refueling trucks, or emergency vehicles. As the plane taxied to the end of the runway we saw the first sign of life. Several hundred uniformed, Kalashnikov-toting Afghans emerged, marching in some semblance of formation onto the field. Press reports had recently claimed that British troops had occupied Bagram. The Afghan honor guard was evidence to the contrary, intended as the Northern Alliance's clear statement of who was in charge.

"Watch out for land mines," the head of my security detail warned as we exited the plane. In Bosnia and Kosovo I had been advised never to walk anywhere that was unpaved. Following that advice was going to be harder in Afghanistan, where little had ever been paved and less remained so.

After completing my inspection of the honor guard, I followed a bit warily in my hosts' footsteps as they led my group toward a motorcade of several dusty, somewhat-dated black Mercedes. The meeting site turned out to be no more than a few hundred yards distant. The cars may have been intended to keep us from straying onto unswept areas, but their principal purpose, I surmised, was to provide a ceremonial aspect to our visit.

Moments later we were escorted into one of the few remaining buildings with its roof intact, the former base hospital. We were shown upstairs into an elongated room where a group of about a dozen men awaited us. At their head sat a dignified older man with a white beard who wore a traditional Afghan robe.

Abdullah introduced me to President Rabbani and, ranged to his side down the length of the room, to the other ministers and generals who formed the Northern Alliance's political and military leadership. Most wore some version of a military uniform, but a few, like Abdullah, were in Western coats and ties. On my side of the room was the much smaller group of military and civilian advisers I had brought from Washington. Hovering in the background were several CIA and U.S. Army Special Forces operatives who had been working with the Afghan leadership for the past several weeks.

The meeting began with a lengthy exchange between Rabbani and I. Our conversation went slowly, as everything had to be translated consecutively. Rabbani had a good interpreter, whom the even more precise Abdullah corrected occasionally. One of the Special Forces troopers translated my responses. Rabbani expressed his gratitude for the American assistance that had permitted the Northern Alliance armies to defeat the Taliban, recover Kabul, and secure control over an increasing proportion of the country. He hoped that the United States would stay and help his country recover from decades of devastating civil war.

I said that the United States recognized its mistake in abandoning Afghanistan following the Soviet Union's withdrawal in 1989. The 9/11 attacks had demonstrated the consequences of such neglect. We Americans would not turn our backs on his country again. Washington appreciated the role that he and his colleagues had played in resisting the Taliban's tyranny. I also conveyed the U.S. government's wish to work with the Northern Alliance to form a new, more broadly based Afghan government, under new leadership, one that could unite the country and secure support from the rest of the international community.

Rabbani accepted all this discourse graciously, without rising to my reference to the need for new leadership. After several exchanges in this same vein, the president took his leave, as Abdullah had advised me he would. His exit had been scripted to give the rest of the Northern Alliance's leadership an opportunity to introduce and unburden themselves and not be inhibited by their nominal chief's presence.

General Fahim, who spoke next, was eager to explain why his troops had occupied Kabul only days after he had promised President Bush that they would not. Washington had been worried that a battle for control of the capital could lead to prolonged urban fighting at great cost to the civilian population, would entrench the Northern Alliance in power, and would increase its opposition throughout the Pashtun south, thereby making the achievement of a more broadly based government more difficult. Pakistan had emphasized these concerns, reasonable enough in the light of Afghanistan's recent history, in the hopes of getting Washington to limit Northern Alliance gains. President Bush had asked the Northern Alliance—and it had agreed—not to occupy the city until Pashtun resistance elements or a United Nations (UN) peacekeeping force could join the alliance in Kabul's liberation and administration.

As it turned out, Fahim explained, the Taliban had decided not to defend Kabul; in fact, Taliban forces had abruptly abandoned the city once their defensive lines on the plains around Bagram had been breached. The Northern Alliance faced the choice of either leaving Kabul to its own devices, with no one to provide for public security, or occupying it themselves. In these circumstances, Fahim said, the likelihood of disorder and ethnic violence seemed greater if the Northern Alliance had stayed out than if it had entered the city. Accordingly, Northern Alliance military and police forces had moved in and secured it. The troops had been well behaved, and there had been no looting or destruction. The city was quiet and the population secure.

I was inclined to accept his explanation at face value, never having thought Washington's stance on the issue very practical. The southern Pashtun resistance movement was not consequential enough to have aided in the city's liberation. Further, the United States, the United Nations, or any other element of the international community was not in any position to assume responsibility for the city's security. Once the Taliban had chosen to abandon its capital, the Northern Alliance leadership had, in my judgment, made the only responsible decision.

In any case, this problem was water under the bridge. I listened sympathetically, expressed understanding, and did not voice the reproaches that Fahim and his colleagues seemed to anticipate.

As interior minister and thus head of the police, Younis Qanooni shared with Fahim responsibility for the capital's security. He too was eager to assure me that the city was in reliable hands, but his main points were more political. He repeated the commitment that Abdullah had provided the previous day, declaring that the Northern Alliance would participate in a conference the United Nations was organizing to form a new Afghan government. He raised a number of questions regarding how that meeting should be organized, where it would be held, and who should be invited. He said the Northern Alliance preferred that the meeting take place in Kabul. He objected to the participation of three different émigré groupings and to their each receiving the same status and numerical participation as the Northern Alliance. He concluded, however, that these were "concerns, not conditions."

Fahim and Qanooni made an interesting contrast. The former, in military combat fatigues, was the image of an Afghan warlord—tough, rough hewn, bearded, and powerfully built. Qanooni was quite the opposite, being slight, clean-shaven, handsome, and rather dapperly dressed in an English-cut tweed jacket, cardigan, and flannel trousers. While Fahim showed no comprehension of English, Qanooni followed each word with lively interest but still required translation.

Having engaged in a brief exchange with each of the military and political leaders present, I was ready to conclude the day's business. I had secured what I had come for, a Northern Alliance commitment to participate in the upcoming conference that would write Afghanistan's interim constitution and name its next government. Further discussion could only raise new problems or qualify existing assurances.

I suggested to Abdullah that we hold a joint press conference. This exercise would allow me to lock in the day's accomplishments. It would also please Washington, which was anxious for evidence that its diplomatic track was catching up to the fast-moving military situation. The publicity also would serve as a useful goad to the other Afghan factions and help accelerate their preparations for the forthcoming conference.

At this point British diplomat Stephen Evans was shown into the room. He was the lead element of the newly reopened British Embassy in Kabul. Earlier in the week a handful of British soldiers had arrived unexpectedly in Bagram, leading the London press to trumpet the United Kingdom's possession of the airfield. This development had greatly annoyed the Northern Alliance authorities, whose forces had been fighting and dying for several years over control of the base and had finally achieved it. One of my tasks was to help smooth over this incident.

I briefed Evans on our discussions, and we agreed that he, Abdullah, and I should speak to the press together. This task proved more difficult than anticipated, for no journalists were in the immediate vicinity. A couple of members of the local CIA team, who had been unobtrusively facilitating the day's events, volunteered to go in search of the fourth estate. They groused good humoredly that arranging press conferences didn't normally fall within their job description.

Eventually three rather surprised Western reporters were produced, cameras at the ready. They duly recorded the return of American and British diplomacy to Afghanistan. Abdullah also reiterated his government's willingness to participate in the prospective UN conference. I cited Qanooni's assurance that the Northern Alliance's several reservations regarding the conference had been expressed as concerns, not conditions, and that I was now confident that the meeting would convene in the near future.

DURING INTERVALS in the morning's discussions, I had seen soldiers on the grounds below our building grilling meat and vegetables over large open fires. I assumed they were preparing their midday meal, but it turned out to be ours. We had entered the holy month of Ramadan, during which Muslims were adjured from eating or drinking from sunrise to sunset. Ours was, therefore, a rather solitary feast. Only General Fahim, a diabetic who was consequently excused from observing the fast, joined us. Abdullah, a dutiful host, also remained. He made polite conversation and insisted that he was not hungry. The atmosphere was slightly strained, though, as we made modest inroads into the copious supply of roasted lamb and other delicacies before us. We trusted that, with sunset, the rest would not go to waste.

At the conclusion of this welcome repast, we climbed into our motorcade for the short drive back to the aircraft. Nearing the plane, I spotted another group of Afghan soldiers approaching in loose formation. This smaller honor guard seemed more ragged in appearance than the first had. These men were bearded, wore native headdresses rather than helmets, and carried an assortment of ponchos, shawls, and other nonregulation items. On close inspection it became evident that they were not, in fact, Afghans but rather American soldiers. They were a contingent of the 5th Special Forces Group that had been operating with the Northern Alliance in the previous several weeks, providing the vital link between Afghan ground units and American airpower. Their leader introduced himself as Col. John Mulholland, the most senior American military officer in Afghanistan at the time. He asked me to say a few words to his men.

Seldom have I felt less equal to an occasion. Standing in the bright midday sun at the end of a battered runway, surrounded by blasted earth and ruined buildings, and with the mountains of Afghanistan rising in the background, this small knot of soldiers had played the crucial role in one of history's swiftest and most decisive military campaigns. I spoke of their achievements, of the American people's admiration and gratitude for them, and of the part that the United States would play in rebuilding the country they had helped liberate. I concluded that while America's role in Afghanistan was just beginning, theirs would never be forgotten.

A few minutes later we were off, on our way back to Tashkent and then to Washington.

2

ONE MORE MISSION

ON A CLEAR, SUNNY, LATE-SUMMER MORNING I watched smoke rise over the Pentagon, listened to radio reports of attacks on the Twin Towers, and, just as thousands of other Americans in Washington and New York, wondered anxiously where my family was. Afghanistan could not have been further from my thoughts. That land did not hold any personal associations for me whatsoever. During thirty-seven years of military and diplomatic service I had lived, served in, or at least visited virtually every region on earth save Central Asia. It was the last place on earth I expected to be sent.

In fact, I did not anticipate being sent anywhere. I was about to retire. In the weeks following September 11, as my State Department colleagues hurried up and down the halls and coped with the manifold diplomatic aspects of the U.S. response to the 9/11 attacks, I spent my days sorting through old papers and contacting prospective new employers. I was, consequently, both available and pleased to receive a call in late October from Under Secretary of State Marc Grossman, the department's third ranking official. Grossman asked whether I would be willing to serve as Secretary of State Colin Powell's envoy to the Afghan opposition. He explained that the military campaign was beginning to gain momentum but that the political track was not keeping pace. America was committed to overthrowing the Taliban regime in Kabul but had, as yet, no clear idea of what group could be put in its place or how to do it. Would I take on this assignment?

Marc did not rehearse my qualifications. I was not familiar with the country, the region, its languages, or its leading personalities. Over the previous decade, however, I had become the department's handyman of choice in the increasingly busy craft of nation-building.

RECONSTRUCTING war-ravaged states was by no means my chosen vocation. I had, quite the contrary, aspired to a traditional diplomatic career, one spent in large cosmopolitan capitals dealing with other well-functioning governments. For more than twenty-five years I had realized this ambition, working in Paris, London, Bonn, and Brussels, rising twice to head the State Department's European Bureau, and serving as the U.S. ambassador to the European Community (EC). With the end of the Cold War, however, the center of gravity for American diplomacy began to shift and my career with it. For me the change had come on a day in late October 1993, when I was asked to take responsibility for managing the U.S. forces' withdrawal from Somalia.

That call too had come out of the blue. It was one of many reverberations flowing from the "Black Hawk Down" incident earlier that month, when eighteen American soldiers lost their lives in a day-long firefight after one of their transport helicopters was shot down and left them stranded in downtown Mogadishu. Secretary of Defense Les Aspin lost his job as a result. The shake-up at the State Department was less drastic. The department sent a new ambassador to Mogadishu. I was asked to take over the "crisis management" function at Washington's end. Some at the administration's senior level saw my lack of African experience as something of a qualification. They felt those experts on the region had failed to avert disaster and that it was time to try something, or at least someone, new.

The decision to withdraw U.S. forces from Somalia in six months had been announced before I assumed my new responsibilities. My job was to arrange a graceful exit, one not burdened by further military or diplomatic setbacks. Accordingly, I spent that time looking for countries that would send soldiers to hold the beachhead while the Americans left and persuading local warlords, including Gen. Mohammed Farah Aideed, the raid's target, not to complicate the U.S. departure.

Within these rather narrow parameters, my mission was entirely successful. American forces departed without further loss or embarrassment while twenty thousand UN peacekeepers stayed behind to lend military and political cover to the U.S. withdrawal. One year later, by which time Somalia had faded from the American headlines, the U.S. Navy sailed back into Mogadishu harbor and lifted the remaining UN troops off the beach.

As an exercise in nation-building, the intervention in Somalia ended in complete failure. As a rehearsal for future similar endeavors, the experience provided President Bill Clinton's new and untried administration a salutary lesson. Those senior officials who survived the experience approached future commitments with considerably more care than they had this one.

Personally, I hoped the end of this operation would allow me to return to more familiar and salubrious climes, but it was not to be. No sooner were U.S. forces out of Somalia than the Clinton administration began to plan for a possible intervention in Haiti. My modest success in helping create the conditions for the military's disengagement from Somalia was somehow seen as qualification for helping arrange an invasion of Haiti. A military coup there in 1991 had ousted the democratically elected president, Jean-Bertrand Aristide. President Clinton was now determined to restore him to power.

Over the next several years, one assignment of this sort led to another. American troops went into Haiti in 1994, into Bosnia in 1995, and into Kosovo in 1999. I became associated with each of these enterprises, acting as the Washington-based troubleshooter responsible for overseeing these interventions' stabilization and reconstruction phases.

All these operations proved highly controversial. President Clinton was criticized for not knowing the difference between foreign policy and social work. Opponents in Congress alleged that incessant nation-building was cutting into the recruitment, retention, and readiness rates of America's armed forces, damaging allegations that turned out to be almost completely groundless. Condoleezza (Condi) Rice, in the run-up to the 2000 elections, wrote that the American military "is not a civilian police force. It is not a political referee. And it is most certainly not designed to build a civilian society." In his televised debate with Vice President Al Gore, George W. Bush said he did not intend to employ American armed forces in such missions in the future.

By the last year of the Clinton administration, I had become assistant secretary of state for Europe. At Secretary Powell's request, I continued in this position for the first half of 2001 while awaiting the selection and confirmation of my successor. In this capacity I participated in several of the new administration's initial policy deliberations, including a meeting among cabinet-level principals to consider whether to pull American troops out of Bosnia.

This issue was hardly the nation's most pressing concern. Things were quiet in both Bosnia and Kosovo. American troop levels had been drawn down steadily in both operations in the past several years, and further reductions were already planned for later in 2001. Having observed half a dozen presidential transitions, however, I knew well enough that neophyte administrations enter office still under the thrall of campaign rhetoric and eager to find easy ways to deliver on sometimes half-baked promises.

Bill Clinton had picked the issue of gays in the military for his first foray into national security policy. It looked as if George Bush would make his mark by backing out of Bosnia.

On the one hand, my having served as President Clinton's senior adviser for the Balkans made the incoming team naturally regard me with some suspicion. On the other hand, Powell, National Security Adviser Rice, and Deputy National Security Adviser Stephen Hadley all knew me well from our time together in prior Republican administrations, and all three were inclined to accord my advice some respect. I had no links, though, to the new team in the Pentagon.

We first debated this Bosnia pullout issue at the subcabinet level, in a National Security Council (NSC) Deputies Committee meeting Steve Hadley chaired. Stephen Cambone, a senior aide to Secretary of Defense Donald Rumsfeld, represented the Defense Department. He complained regretfully that the Clinton administration had intervened to stop the civil war in Bosnia too early. If the killing there had been allowed to continue awhile longer, the parties would have become exhausted, one would have been beaten into submission, and the subsequent process of peacekeeping would have been easier. While arguably true, his assessment ignored both the humanitarian and broader geopolitical reasons for the intervention. In any case, it was not germane to our discussion, since even Cambone was not proposing that we allow the fighting to resume.

I did not waste any time defending the Clinton administration's policy before what I knew was an unsympathetic audience. Instead, I suggested the new administration should take credit for a nearly 50 percent cut in American troop strength in Bosnia planned for later that year. Why jeopardize a successful operation by an abrupt and total withdrawal, I argued, when troop numbers were already on the desired glide path?

Don Rumsfeld, however, would have no truck with half measures. He wanted a complete and immediate American withdrawal. Accordingly, we gathered again a few days later in the White House Situation Room at the NSC Principals'—that is, cabinet—level. Condi Rice was the chair, and Vice President Dick Cheney, Rumsfeld, and Powell were all in attendance.

Eight years earlier, it had fallen to Colin Powell, as the then-JCS chairman, to divert the Clinton administration's "gays in the military" express train onto the "don't ask, don't tell" siding. Now, as George Bush's secretary of state, he found himself once again standing between a new administration and an ill-conceived, or at least untimely, campaign promise. Powell avoided engaging Rumsfeld on the military case for continuing a North Atlantic Treaty Organization (NATO) presence in Bosnia and left it to me to carry that argument. Instead, Powell took his stand on the purely political and diplomatic grounds that the United States was committed to its NATO partners to see this mission through to completion, and whatever the new Pentagon leadership might think, those partners did not believe that the mission had yet been accomplished.

Driving back to the State Department together after the meeting, I told Powell that his predecessor, Madeleine Albright, had been uncomfortable arguing military matters with the secretary of defense and sometimes let that task fall to me; however, I didn't expect to do the same under his leadership. Powell responded that he had the opposite problem. It wasn't that he feared knowing too little about defense matters, but too much. Any effort on his part to engage the Pentagon leadership on military issues would only be resented and rebuffed.

Powell's position prevailed in this particular dispute. Several weeks later we both traveled to Brussels for his initial encounter with the other NATO foreign ministers. They had gotten wind of the Washington debate over U.S. troop levels in the Balkans and were relieved to receive Powell's assurance that "we went in together, and we will come out together."

SEVERAL MONTHS later I turned the European Bureau over to my successor. I was pleased to have held the United States to its Balkan commitments, but I left certain the administration would not need an experienced nation-builder anytime soon. Yet after only a few months, it was about to invade Afghanistan, a country some ten times bigger than Bosnia. And once again, I was invited to take a hand in the associated diplomacy. I quickly agreed. Grossman asked me to tell no one and sit tight for a couple of days while Powell cleared the appointment with the White House and the Department of Defense (DOD). Two days extended into nearly a week, but eventually Grossman called and said that all boxes had been checked, and those currently working on Afghanistan in the State Department, DOD, and the White House had been alerted to expect a new team member.

As usual, my initial challenges were administrative. Long experience in the government had taught me that space, staff, funding, and authority would come only at someone else's expense. Before I could get to work, I needed to determine where I would be housed, who would pay my bills, how to recruit a staff, what my sphere of activity was, and how my responsibilities would relate to those of others already working on Afghanistan. Working out these irksome issues proved no easier than the previous times I had suddenly been parachuted into an ongoing crisis management team in which all the seats were already occupied.

In this case I needed to define the nature of my duties further. What exactly did "envoy to the Afghan opposition" mean? That opposition was highly dispersed. Some of its leaders were in Afghanistan fighting the Taliban. Others had taken up residency in neighboring states, including Pakistan, Iran, Tajikistan, and Uzbekistan. Still others were located further afield, living in Western Europe and the United States.

Richard Armitage, the deputy secretary of state, wanted to pack me off immediately to Central Asia, where I would orbit Afghanistan more or less indefinitely and meet when and where I could with those opposition figures I could find. This arrangement would at least give the appearance of active diplomacy, and this appearance, I learned, was not a negligible consideration. British prime minister Tony Blair had appointed his own personal envoy to the Afghan opposition several weeks earlier; thus, the contrast between a visible British engagement and the absence of any comparable American diplomatic activity had already become a sore point within the administration. In fact, in some measure, my appointment was a response to Blair's initiative.

I was reluctant, however, to move to the end of a twelve thousand–mile telephone line just to provide Washington with a series of diplomatic photo opportunities. My conception of the job reflected my experience over the past decade, when I had helped craft the policies that I then represented in the field. I wanted to be based in Washington and help write the instructions I would be carrying, that is, to participate in the administration's policy process as well as to act as its messenger.

Grossman was sympathetic to my vision of the job. He recognized that more work needed to be done in Washington and New York before regional diplomacy could produce anything useful. Unfortunately, Armitage was Grossman's superior and Colin Powell's closest adviser. He wanted me to leave as soon as possible and to stay in Central Asia indefinitely.

Procrastination, compromise, and the force of circumstances eventually resolved this issue in my favor. It was agreed that I would leave for Central Asia only after accompanying Colin Powell the following week to a meeting in New York, where he and the foreign ministers from all of Afghanistan's neighboring states would launch an internationally backed process for forming that country's next government. From New York, I would make an initial circuit of Central Asia and then return to Washington before deciding where to be based.

Over the next few days I managed to scrounge an office, a telephone, and the beginnings of a staff. My longtime personal assistant, Brenda Kinser-Kidane, who had worked with me on several previous assignments, proved ready to take on yet another. Craig Karp, one of the few Foreign Service officers (FSOs) with experience in Afghanistan, joined our team.

Under normal circumstances, policy toward Afghanistan fell within the purview of the head of the State Department's Bureau of South Asian Affairs, and in the White House, it came under the senior NSC official responsible for the Middle East. Christina Rocca, a former CIA and congressional staffer, had the first of those positions while Zalmay Khalilzad, a former RAND analyst with prior experience at both the State and Defense departments, held the second. Under the enormous work pressures generated after the 9/11 attacks, however, their authority had been diluted. Colin Powell had given the head of his Policy Planning Staff, Richard Haass, a somewhat loosely defined role in coordinating Afghan policy, and Rice had done something similar within the NSC staff. Thus Frank Miller, a career civil servant with several decades of experience inside DOD, had responsibility for coordinating all the military aspects of the Afghan campaign while Khalilzad retained responsibility for the political side.

Of these individuals I had not worked with Rocca in previous administrations. She immediately impressed me as knowledgeable, businesslike, personable, and level headed. Her lack of prior diplomatic experience and her office's size, by far the smallest of the State Department's six regional bureaus, limited her impact somewhat. The former deficit she made up quickly, but the latter would prove a permanent limitation. She simply lacked the staff, the budget, and the authority to handle the myriad issues associated with Afghanistan's liberation and reconstruction.

Any effort to stabilize post-Taliban Afghanistan would need, at a minimum, to engage all six of that country's neighbors, but only one, Pakistan, fell within the jurisdiction of Rocca's South Asia Bureau. The European Bureau was responsible for relations with the three states north of Afghanistan, the Middle Eastern Bureau for Iran, and the East Asian Bureau for China. This compartmentalization was why, in the aftermath of 9/11, the Policy Planning Staff had been assigned the task of coordinating policy among all the relevant bureaus.

Richard Haass and I had worked together on numerous occasions in the previous twenty years. Throughout the Gulf War he had held Khalilzad's position, the Middle East portfolio within the White House, and it served as excellent preparation for his duties under Powell. Although Haass's office was no larger than Rocca's, it did have a global perspective and more varied policy expertise, but lacked authority to instruct overseas missions or to conduct relations with foreign governments, his Policy Planning Staff having even less operational capacity than the South Asian Bureau had.

Among the senior officials in Washington dealing with Afghanistan, Zalmay Khalilzad was in some respects the most qualified. In earlier Republican administrations, Khalilzad had served in both the State and Defense departments and had worked for Paul Wolfowitz, who was now Secretary

Rumsfeld's top deputy. Khalilzad had also headed Rumsfeld's transition team at DOD during the weeks between the 2000 election and the inauguration. A first-generation Afghan American who had spent his youth, into high school, in Kabul, Khalilzad had maintained his connections with Afghanistan and, over the years, become acquainted with many personalities in and outside its government. He was the only participant in the Washington policy process who had firsthand knowledge of that country and its leadership and the only one who could speak to the Afghan leaders in their own language.

Khalilzad, however, had largely ceded responsibility for managing the interagency process to Frank Miller, his NSC colleague. Miller chaired the relevant interagency committee, but that group was focused almost exclusively on ensuring that the U.S. military buildup in the region proceeded smoothly. This division of labor, while sensible in light of both these officials' expertise, created a gap in the interagency management process. Miller was in a position to get things done, but he did not direct his efforts toward our particular problem. While Khalilzad was focused on our issues, he did not have the capacity to readily translate ideas into collective action.

While Rocca, Haass, Khalilzad, and Miller all brought considerable experience and talent to the policy-making table, there was no hierarchy among them. No one was in a position to direct or even coordinate the others' activities. No one had the capacity to convene the others, collect their views, and provide agreed (or disagreed) recommendations to the president's cabinet-level advisers. Thus the burden of forging agreed guidance fell on the cabinet-level principals themselves, all of whom had many other competing responsibilities. This arrangement stood in sharp contrast to the pattern established for handling similar matters within the previous administration. Badly burned by the experience of Somalia, where poor staff work in Washington had contributed to the debacle in Mogadishu, the Clinton administration thereafter made it a rule to appoint a single official at the subcabinet level, sometimes at the State Department and sometimes at the White House, to oversee all the policy aspects of any military intervention. This practice had eventually been formalized in a Presidential Decision (PD) memorandum. On entering office the Bush administration had decided to allow that particular directive to lapse.

At this point, Rocca, Haass, Khalilzad, and Miller did not have any fundamental policy disagreements. No one in the Bush administration wished to see an American military occupation of Afghanistan on the model of post–World War II Germany or Japan. Neither did anyone want to see an international administration on the model of Bosnia and Kosovo. Instead, everyone hoped the Taliban could be succeeded by a broadly based, moderate Afghan regime that would unify the country, reassure its neighbors, and cooperate with the United States in stamping out any residual terrorist threat. Determining how to achieve that outcome was the problem.

The desire to minimize both the U.S. and international roles in Afghanistan's post-Taliban governance had several rationales. First, the Afghans had repeatedly resisted foreign domination, having twice driven out the British in 1841 and 1881 and then the Soviets in 1989. Next, the Bush administration was on record as opposing the American military's participation in nation-building. Finally, it was equally skeptical about the capacity of the United Nations to undertake such operations.

Meanwhile, throughout the administration officials recognized that the Northern Alliance was not sufficiently representative to provide a stable post-Taliban regime. As its name implied, this resistance movement had drawn its strength from the Dari-speaking Tajik, Uzbek, and Hazara populations concentrated in the northern half of the country. By contrast, the Taliban came from the Pashto-speaking communities of the south and east. The latter was ethnically and linguistically linked to the Pashtun tribes on the other side of Pakistan's North-West frontier. Lacking any recent census, the exact proportion represented by any one of these groups was in dispute, but the Pashtuns were irrefutably the largest community, making up somewhere between 40 and 60 percent of the total Afghan population.

The challenge, therefore, was twofold: to find Pashtun leaders who retained credibility in their community and who had not been contaminated by collaborating with the Taliban, and then to persuade the Northern Alliance leadership to share power with these figures.

3

GETTING SET

I SPENT THE NEXT WEEK meeting with the many people whose help I would need to complete my mission. On hearing about my appointment, several old friends sought me out also. One was John Negroponte, recently installed as the U.S. ambassador to the United Nations. We had lunch at John's club, located a few blocks north of the White House. Our conversation opened with reminiscences of an earlier time together. We had both been members of the American delegation to the 1968 Vietnam peace talks in Paris, where we had had the opportunity to watch several of our country's most experienced negotiators in action. These men included our chief, Averell Harriman, who had served as Franklin Delano Roosevelt's emissary to the Kremlin throughout World War II, and Harriman's deputy, Cyrus Vance, who later became Jimmy Carter's secretary of state. The delegation's most senior career diplomat was Philip Habib, whose warm heart, brash manner, loud voice, and fierce determination became legendary within the Foreign Service. Among the delegation's more junior officers was Richard Holbrooke, another rising star in American diplomacy.

Harriman was a somewhat distant figure. FDR's successor as governor of New York, he still preferred to be addressed by that title than by ambassador. Less formally, he was also known as "the Crocodile" for his tenacity in bureaucratic battle. Then pushing eighty years old, this scion of a nineteenth-century railroad baron still insisted on taking the stairs, two steps at a time, instead of elevators whenever possible. Vance was somewhat more approach-able. Rumor had it that President Lyndon Johnson had assigned the soft-spoken and understated corporate lawyer to our delegation to keep an eye on Harriman, who was considered too willful and independent to be entirely trusted. For the delegation's younger members, Habib was our taskmaster and father figure, and he played both roles with great panache.

Negroponte, Holbrooke, and I were all in our late twenties, but John and Richard were already several steps ahead of me in the State Department's hi-erarchy. They entered the service more or less directly from university whereas I had spent several years in the navy first. Both of them had passed much of that time in Saigon, as political officers in the embassy unit Habib headed. Both were consequently much more familiar than I with the issues on which we were working.

Negroponte and Holbrooke, so alike in experience, had wholly dissimi-lar personalities. Even as a junior officer, Holbrooke was hot tempered, flam-boyant, by turns warmly engaging and infuriatingly abrasive, and always eager for the limelight. By contrast, Negroponte had a cool, wry, and slightly patri-cian manner and showed little interest in media attention. In later years both men had advanced to the top of their profession. Since Paris we had crossed paths occasionally. In the early 1990s from a position in the White House, I had overseen a negotiation Negroponte conducted. A few years later I suc-ceeded Holbrooke as the Clinton administration's chief Balkan negotiator. A big part of my job had been to sustain the implementation of the Bosnian peace agreement known as General Framework Agreement for Peace in Bosnia and Herzegovina, or Dayton Accords, that he had brokered at the 1995 Day-ton conference. Subsequently, I also succeeded Holbrooke as assistant secre-tary of state for Europe, by which time he had become our representative to the United Nations, the most prestigious American ambassadorship. In 2001 Negroponte had succeeded Holbrooke in that same position.

John now suggested my new responsibilities resembled those Harriman and Vance had faced on their arrival in Paris thirty-three years earlier. I took this observation more as a graceful compliment than a serious analogy. Negroponte insisted, however, that the negotiating skills we had observed then were what the current circumstances demanded. I responded that the prob-lems Holbrooke faced at Dayton might offer a closer comparison.

As our meal arrived, we moved on to more practical matters. We discussed what role the United Nations could play in helping us pull together a new Afghan government. For weeks American officials had urged leaders from the various Afghan opposition factions to come together, resolve their differences, and select a successor regime so that it could be ready to assume power as soon as the Taliban was overthrown. The Northern Alliance leadership and former king Zahir Shah's supporters, the two most significant opposition groups, had agreed to meet but found one excuse after another to avoid doing so. The fault lay mostly with the Northern Alliance leaders, who were best positioned to seize territory once the American bombing campaign gained momentum. They seemed in no great hurry to engage in power-sharing arrangements with émigré figures who had no forces on the ground and consequently had played little role in toppling the Taliban.

Absent substantial external pressure, a meaningful rapprochement between these groups seemed unlikely. We needed some catalytic event just to get them in the same room together. Rather than wait for the Afghans to coalesce, therefore, I suggested that the United Nations take the initiative and call a conference at which a new Afghan government would be formed. Each of the Afghan factions would be told either to show up or to forfeit its role in forming that government.

Negroponte agreed that this convening role was a natural one for the United Nations. Off and on for more than a decade UN officials had been seeking to mediate an end to Afghanistan's endless civil war. UN humanitarian agencies had also been active in helping the millions of refugees the conflict produced. As a result, almost alone among international institutions and major governments, the United Nations had maintained a presence in Afghanistan and was familiar with most of the major political figures in and outside the government and the country.

The top UN official responsible for Afghanistan was Lakhdar Brahimi, a former Algerian foreign minister and longtime confidant of UN secretary general Kofi Annan. The many American officials with whom he had worked over the years regarded Brahimi well. I had first met him in 1995 when Brahimi headed a UN peacekeeping mission in Haiti. We quickly formed an effective working relationship and became good friends.

Our first task had been to manage the handoff from the American-led multinational coalition that had occupied Haiti and restored its elected president to a UN-run, blue-helmeted peacekeeping operation. We were familiar with the similar transition from U.S. to UN leadership that had taken place in Somalia two years earlier and had not gone well. Indeed, President Clinton and UN secretary general Boutros Boutros-Ghali were both still trying to recover from that disaster, and each saw Haiti as an opportunity to restore his reputation for competent nation-building. Brahimi and I were their chosen instruments.

The handoff from U.S. to UN authority was, accordingly, meticulously prepared from both sides. We greatly reduced American troop strength, although the U.S. contingent remained the largest element of the new UN force, and an American general still exercised command but under Brahimi's oversight. For another eighteen months Brahimi and I worked closely together, as UN and U.S. officials labored to organize national elections and to install new local governments, a new parliament, and a new president. Then American troops left, and a couple of years later so did the rest of the UN peacekeeping force. These departures proved premature. Most of the reforms introduced during the brief international presence began to unravel. Brahimi and I had organized what was regarded at the time a model operation, but Washington and UN politics at that stage could not sustain the longer-term commitment that might have yielded more enduring results. Brahimi had nevertheless established a reputation in Washington for prudence, competence, and an ability to work well with American officials.

Negroponte and I discussed how the United Nations could best kick start the process of forming an Afghan government. A first step was already under way. One week hence Secretary General Annan would convene a meeting that would bring together all of Afghanistan's neighbors and the two other powers—namely, the United States and Russia—that had used Afghan territory over the years as a battleground in their proxy wars. These representatives would endorse a proposal for the United Nations to convene a conference of Afghan opposition leaders, empowering that meeting to pick the next Afghan government. Brahimi and I would then work together to ensure that the right mix of Afghans would attend and agree on an interim constitution and the composition of a new government.

Assuming we were successful, a UN Security Council resolution could then give the results of this conference formal weight. Of course, American military power would provide the primary impulse for this diplomacy, but the Bush administration was wisely intent on avoiding any appearance of occupying Afghanistan or selecting its new government. UN leadership and broad multilateral support, therefore, would be vital to achieving a sustainable outcome without involving a massive influx of American military manpower.

FOLLOWING MY LUNCH with Negroponte, two other former colleagues called on me—the American ambassadors to Pakistan and to India. Wendy Chamberlin, the U.S. envoy in Islamabad, sought to impress upon me how important and difficult had been the policy shift Pakistani president Pervez Musharraf initiated immediately after 9/11, when he had promised to cut his government's links to the Taliban and support an American military offensive designed to bring down that regime. The Taliban was, after all, largely a Pakistani creation. Pakistani officials remained highly concerned about the kind of Afghan government that would result from this American intervention, as Pakistan and the Northern Alliance had been on opposite sides of the Afghan civil war for nearly a decade. Islamabad feared, reasonably enough, that a Northern Alliance–dominated Afghan regime would prove hostile to Pakistan's interests and favorable to those of India.

Chamberlin urged me to visit Islamabad soon and consult its officials closely before I ventured any further in Afghan diplomacy. She invited me to stay with her during my visit. She cautioned, however, that she would brook no effort to circumvent her authority over U.S. diplomacy in or about Pakistan.

This warning struck me as a bit defensive, considering that I had only been named to my new post a couple of days earlier and had certainly done nothing to provoke suspicion. As I learned more about the history of America's engagement in that region, the reason for her concern became clear. When the Soviets invaded Afghanistan in 1979, Pakistan had become a crossroads for covert operations and secret diplomacy directed toward Afghanistan. I was not the first special envoy Washington sent out for this purpose. Several of my predecessors had seriously disagreed with our embassy in Pakistan, whose first priority was to maintain good relations with its host country and not its neighbor. What was good for Afghanistan was not necessarily good for Pakistan and vice versa. Indeed, Pakistan and Afghanistan generally had poor relations until the Taliban's arrival. Centering our Afghan diplomacy so heavily on and in Pakistan had thus inevitably skewed U.S. policy over the years and had created tensions between those envoys responsible for the U.S. relationship with Afghanistan and Pakistan.

Robert (Bob) Blackwill, Bush's newly installed envoy to New Delhi, also visited me. Twenty-seven years earlier he had recruited me to succeed him as an aide to Helmut Sonnenfeld, who was then Secretary of State Henry Kissinger's top adviser on Soviet and European affairs. Three years later he again arranged for me to follow him into the political section of our embassy in London, one of the most sought-after postings in the Foreign Service. A decade later while he was in George H. W. Bush's White House and I was in James Baker's State Department, we worked together on the talks leading to Germany's unification. Another associate in that diplomatic campaign was Condoleezza Rice, then a Soviet expert working for Blackwill.

Bob had left government service almost immediately after Germany's unification and assumed a post at Harvard University. He and Rice had eventually become advisers to George W. Bush in his 2000 run for the presidency. Blackwill's reward was the embassy in New Delhi. He was determined that it would not be a sinecure. India was a rising democratic power, and Blackwill wanted to transform its relationship with the United States, traditionally rather distant and mutually suspicious, to reflect this new reality.

I had heard some of Blackwill's thoughts several months earlier, before he left for his new post. Since then he had made headway in getting both governments' leaders to take each other more seriously. The 9/11 attacks had thrown a major roadblock in his path when Washington's attention turned almost exclusively to the war in Afghanistan. Pakistani cooperation was essential to prosecuting that war. India's was not. Thus Pakistan, heretofore an international pariah and target of U.S. sanctions, was suddenly Washington's most important ally in the war on terror. Relations with India, only recently seen in Washington as a democratic counterweight to a rising China, were now on the administration's back burner.

Blackwill was considerably frustrated with this turn of events. He stressed to me the important role India had been playing in opposing the Taliban and its resultant influence with the Afghan opposition. He urged that I visit New Delhi soon and consult closely with the Indian government on the U.S. approach to post-Taliban Afghanistan. I promised to do so.

Gen. Wesley Clark also called me and offered his assistance. Before becoming NATO's supreme allied commander in Europe (SACEUR) in the late 1990s, General Clark had served as Richard Holbrooke's military adviser during the Dayton Accords, the negotiations that ended the Bosnian civil war. Clark was ready to perform the same service for me. I was impressed by his desire to serve, even in a relatively subordinate position, during this time of national crisis, but I also saw considerable difficulty in accepting his offer. Even within the Clinton administration, Clark had been a controversial figure whom some warmly admired and others roundly criticized. Unfortunately for him, most of his admirers had been in the State Department and his critics in the Pentagon.

Clark and I had first worked together on planning the American-led intervention in Haiti in 1994. The following year he helped Holbrooke fashion the Dayton Accords. Rewarded with a fourth star and promoted to command all American and allied forces throughout Europe, Clark then directed the agreement's military implementation. As SACEUR he also pressed for a tougher Western response to Serbia's ethnic cleansing in Kosovo. In the subsequent NATO air campaign, Clark managed to achieve NATO's objectives without losing a single soldier, sailor, or airman; however, he had also antagonized his immediate civilian and military superiors. They announced his replacement as SACEUR only weeks after the war's successful conclusion.

If Clark had been controversial in the Clinton Pentagon, that building's current leaders were even less likely to welcome his return. The Bush administration widely regarded both the Dayton Accords and the Kosovo air war as "anti-models," the former because it committed American troops to an open-ended peacekeeping mission and the latter because the United States allowed its allies some share in decision making. The new leadership in Washington was eager to avoid repeating either of these mistakes.

In mid-1999, senior air force officers, frustrated by the Kosovo air campaign's slow pace, had urged that they be authorized to attack civil infrastructure targets in and around the Serbian capital of Belgrade. Clark had refused. No matter how many bridges and power plants were destroyed, prematurely unleashing the U.S. Air Force in this manner would have broken the NATO alliance and thereby would have handed Slobodan Milosevic an unqualified victory. Nevertheless, much of the American military establishment, as well as many of the Clinton administration's political opponents, had bought into this line of argument. As a result, the new team, always eager to differentiate itself from its predecessors, had already rebuffed NATO's offer of aid in Afghanistan and turned away most allied efforts to contribute troops or aircraft. The Bush administration was determined to avoid any repetition of "war by committee," as it derisively characterized the Kosovo campaign.

In this atmosphere, I realized any effort to bring Clark on to my negotiating team would provoke immediate resistance from the Pentagon and the White House. Thus, I regretfully declined the general's offer. Powell subsequently confirmed that I had made the right decision.

THE AMERICAN general exercising Clark's responsibilities for the current war was Tommy Franks, who headed the U.S. Central Command (CENTCOM). His headquarters (HQ) was located, somewhat improbably, in Tampa, Florida, which was just about as far as one could get from Afghanistan and still be on the same planet. Four days after taking up my new post, I flew down to meet him. On a warm, muggy Sunday afternoon I drove through the tree-shaded streets of this quiet Gulf Coast town. The rigors of an approaching Afghan winter seemed distant indeed.

Tampa is also some distance from Washington. The U.S. military establishment regards this separation as a good thing. Regional commanders like Franks are encouraged to communicate directly with American ambassadors in their area of responsibility but discouraged from doing the same with Washington-based officials. Wesley Clark had revealed to me that an extreme example of this enforced distancing occurred during the Kosovo air campaign, when his Pentagon superiors had expressly forbidden him to initiate contact with anyone in the State Department or the White House. Clark could take calls from Washington, but he was not permitted to originate them. All his communications had to go through his superiors—Secretary of Defense Bill Cohen and Chairman of the Joint Chiefs Hugh Shelton—and neither of these officials shared Clark's views on the war's conduct. Whereas Clark, like Secretary of State Albright, favored employing U.S. and European ground forces if necessary to eject the Serbs from Kosovo, Cohen and Shelton did not. These officials wanted no collusion between Clark and his possible allies in the State Department and the White House.

During the Gulf War, Franks's predecessor, Gen. Norman Schwarzkopf, had commanded the coalition from a forward headquarters in Saudi Arabia, whence he had given regular press briefings and quickly became the public face of the war. Clark had also commanded NATO forces in Kosovo from his HQ in Europe. He too was a highly visible figure, until JCS chairman Shelton called him to relay Secretary of Defense Cohen's orders to "get his f——— face off television." Perhaps recalling Clark's fate, Franks was keeping a low public profile. He stayed off television and left public commentary on the war to the secretary of defense.

Arranging my visit with Franks had proved more complicated than I had anticipated. On learning about my proposed meeting with Franks, Richard Haass, the head of Policy Planning at the State Department, decided to come along. His involvement led Peter Rodman, the assistant secretary of defense responsible for Afghanistan, to ask whether he could join me as well. At first I somewhat resented the implied need to be chaperoned. On reflection, however, I realized they simply wanted to gain greater insight into Franks's intentions. As an emissary who would soon be dispatched to Franks's area of responsibility, I was the sort of civilian official with whom regional commanders were encouraged to maintain contact. Haass and Rodman, as Washington-based civilians outside his chain of command, were not. Had either proposed to visit Tampa on his own, eyebrows would have been raised. My trip offered an unobjectionable excuse for them to see Franks.

The general received us in his office. To my surprise there were no maps, PowerPoint slides, or attendant staff, the usual accompaniments to a military briefing. It was a good sign. Franks assumed we were aware of the general situation and spoke directly of his intended course of action. He talked about seizing an airfield in country and noted that Bagram, once the Soviet Union's most important air base, now lay within reach in the no-man's-land between Northern Alliance and Taliban forces north of Kabul. He also discussed putting American troops in the south, where the Taliban did not face any serious local resistance. U.S. Marines currently embarked on ships in the Bay of Bengal were, he said, the likely candidates for this task.

As he was speaking a colonel hurried into the room. "We have Karzai," he reported. "His helo is just crossing the frontier."

Franks nodded. Turning to us, he explained that Hamid Karzai was a Pashtun resistance commander who had been leading a small band of insurgents into southern Afghanistan. He had come under attack from Taliban forces and radioed for help. Surrounded and about to be overrun, Karzai had been plucked out, just moments earlier, by a helicopter-borne American rescue squad. He was now on his way back into Pakistan.

"We didn't want a second Abdul Haq incident," Franks commented. He was referring to another Pashtun resistance leader whom the Taliban had captured, tortured, and killed a week earlier. Haq had been a mujahideen commander during the Soviet occupation, and in that campaign he had lost a foot. Eager to get into this latest fight, Haq and a handful of followers had entered Afghanistan against the CIA's advice. Like Karzai, he had quickly been detected, surrounded, and threatened with capture. He too had radioed for help, but none had been available. The CIA had fired a Hellfire missile from an overhead drone against his attackers, but it had otherwise been unable to effect his rescue. Unlike Haq, Karzai had official American backing for his effort. Both incidents illustrated the difficulty of mounting effective resistance to the Taliban in the southern and eastern parts of Afghanistan.

Franks promised full support for my mission. He wanted to keep the lightest possible American footprint in Afghanistan. The faster we could establish and install a successor regime, the easier it would be for him to focus on hunting down remaining al Qaeda and Taliban elements. Franks also said that he was coming under increased pressure from both the media and his masters in Washington to show results.

"I know the feeling," I replied, recalling how everyone associated with the Kosovo air campaign had faced mounting criticism as weeks of bombing did not diminish the Serbs' resolve. "Just make sure that every day is a little worse for the Taliban than the day before, and one morning you will wake up to find them gone," I suggested.

To my surprise, Franks heartily agreed. Some military men react badly to incrementalism of this sort. In this case, however, he had little choice. Haass, Rodman, and I flew back to Washington that same evening.

THE FOLLOWING morning I drove out to CIA headquarters, which is located in a complex of modern buildings sprawled across several wooded acres in Langley, Virginia, along the Potomac River. John McLaughlin, the agency's deputy director, met me there and introduced me to several of his colleagues.

John and I had each spent several decades in our respective agencies' European divisions and were well acquainted. In the late 1990s I had worked closely with both John and his chief, George Tenet, on matters related to the Balkans. Under Tenet and McLaughlin the agency spent less time second-guessing policy makers and put more effort into providing constructive advice and assisting them in obtaining their policy objectives. Their inclination to work with rather than against the grain of administration policy eventually became a source of criticism, especially when the policy concerned was the invasion of Iraq, but it had served the United States well in the Balkans and was doing so now in Afghanistan.

I asked McLaughlin to attach one of his officers to my staff and urged him to choose the individual carefully. I needed someone who could tap into the flow of intelligence, keep me apprised on the war's progress, and put me in touch with key Afghan leaders operating inside a country where we had no diplomats and, as yet, almost no soldiers. An agency officer would be my only link to the Afghan opposition's most important elements, those who were actually inside Afghanistan mounting resistance to the Taliban.

McLaughlin promised to find someone good and turned me over to his colleagues to discuss Afghanistan's situation. The first briefer was a member of the agency's paramilitary arm. This element of the clandestine service had been active through the eighties in Afghanistan and in Central America but had seen little action in the subsequent decade. Fortunately, the agency had retained a core group of people who both understood Afghanistan and knew how to support irregular warfare. These clandestine service officers now spearheaded the American response to 9/11.

Listening, I was impressed by the scope and speed of the agency's response to 9/11. Several teams already were in country, doling out money to Afghan commanders and mapping static Taliban targets for American strike aircraft. CIA officers were also preparing the way for the insertion of U.S. Special Forces. These highly trained solders would be equipped with long-range laser designation devices that would help American aircraft hit moving targets with precision munitions.

In the northern half of the country the agency had operatives assigned to each of the major warlords: Ismail Khan in the west, near the border with Iran; Abdul Rashid Dostum with the Uzbek troops; Ustad Atta Mohammed with the Tajiks in the north, near the border with Uzbekistan; and Fahim Khan in the northeast, between Tajikistan and Kabul. Fahim was nominally in overall command.

Throughout the south, resistance to the Taliban was much less developed. Pashtuns heavily populated this part of Afghanistan and the other side of the Pakistan border. The Pashtuns spoke their own language, Pashto, which is distinct from the variant of Persian most of the people in the north spoke. The largest of Afghanistan's ethnicities, Pashtuns often claimed to represent more than 60 percent of the population; however, others argued that they made up no more than 40 percent. The then-current edition of the CIA's *World Factbook*, in its listing for Afghanistan, assigned them 38 percent of the population. Without a completed census and after millions of people were killed or driven out of the country in recent decades, no one could validate these conflicting claims. What was certain was that the Pashtuns had dominated most Afghan governments going back several centuries and therefore regarded it as their birthright. Many Pashtuns also believed the tribal areas of adjacent Pakistan were rightfully part of Afghanistan and tended to count that population in their total. Since more Pashtuns lived in Pakistan than in Afghanistan, their inclusion naturally inflated the Pashtuns' numbers considerably.

The Taliban had arisen among this Pashtun population with the Pakistani Inter-Services Intelligence (ISI) Directorate's support. The CIA was now trying to stir up resistance within this same community, but so far it had met with only limited success. It would be a long time, if ever, before a non-Taliban southern competitor to the Northern Alliance could emerge.

I was pleasantly surprised by the candor with which McLaughlin and his colleagues spoke of their efforts in and around Afghanistan. Getting information about CIA covert operations is normally quite difficult. Given the agency's desire to protect its sources and cover its tracks, it sharply limits information sharing with other cabinet departments and even with White House staff. In this instance I encountered little reticence. On reflection, the reason was pretty clear: this war was open, not covert. Neither the United States nor the Afghan resistance needed to keep their relationship secret. The CIA was in the lead because it had the contacts, familiarity with the terrain, and ready money and not because the operation had to be kept quiet.

THE FOLLOWING DAY I called on Paul Wolfowitz, Rumsfeld's top deputy at the Pentagon. He and I had served together in two of the previous Republican administrations. Although we were never close and sometime differed on issues, he was always a friendly and courteous interlocutor. My main purpose for this call was to ensure that the Defense Department was comfortable with my mission and prepared to assist me. I also asked Wolfowitz to name someone to my team who could keep him apprised of our progress and relay requests for help as needed. In addition, I wanted his reaction to the possibility of deploying an international peacekeeping force to Kabul. It was all but inevitable that the Northern Alliance would take the capital once the Taliban was expelled. The last time the former had controlled Kabul, bitter fighting had broken out, leaving much of the city in ruins. Even if we could avoid such slaughter, Pashtun opposition figures, fearful of politically motivated coercion or worse still, elimination, would be reluctant to return to a Northern Alliance–controlled Kabul.

I anticipated Defense Department resistance to any substantial peacekeeping mission and therefore approached this subject gingerly, not wanting to provoke the wrong answer. Rather than ask a direct question, I simply mentioned the likelihood that elements of the Afghan opposition would call for such a force. Wolfowitz acknowledged that this request could arise and did not express a negative attitude. I took his response as an indication that, even if not enthusiastic, the Pentagon would at least prove acquiescent to such a move and would not block it. It was as much guidance as I needed for the moment.

BACK AT THE STATE Department I went to see the assistant secretary for the Middle East, Bill Burns. His bureau handled America's relations, or rather non-relations, with Afghanistan's second-most-influential neighbor, Iran. While Pakistan had been the Taliban's chief source of support, Iran had been the Northern Alliance's largest backer.

If there are two countries in the world with good reasons to hate each other, they are Iran and America. In 1979 Iranian revolutionaries had seized the American Embassy in Tehran and held its staff hostage for fifteen months. The revolutionary Iranian regime was subsequently implicated both in the 1983 attack on a U.S. Marine barracks in Beirut, Lebanon, that killed 241 American servicemen and dozens of French military and in the 1996 bombing of a U.S. Air Force barracks in Saudi Arabia that killed 19 and injured 500. Iran subsequently ceased to go after American targets, but it continued to support groups in Lebanon and occupied Palestine that conducted attacks on Israel.

Iranians, for their part, also had an imposing set of grievances. In 1953 the CIA had helped instigate a coup against Mohammed Mossadeq's democratically elected government and installed in its place the autocratic regime of Mohammed Reza Pahlavi, Shah of Iran. After the 1979 revolution overthrew the Shah, the United States imposed an embargo on trade with Iran. In 1980 Saddam Hussein launched an invasion of Iran, and during the resulting eight-year war, which killed some 500,000 Iranians, the United States worked with the region's Sunni states and provided various forms of support to Iraq, the aggressor state. Further, when Hussein's forces used poison gas against Iranian troops, the United States did not protest. In 1988 the U.S. Navy shot down an Iranian civil airliner flying over the Persian Gulf, having mistaken it for a hostile military aircraft, and killed 290 innocent crew members and passengers.

Iran and the United States now found themselves on the same side in Afghanistan, opposing the Taliban and al Qaeda and backing the Northern Alliance. Iranian antagonism toward the Taliban had several roots. The Taliban and al Qaeda preached a form of Sunni fundamentalism opposed to the Shia version the Iranian ayatollahs purveyed, and the Taliban actively repressed Afghanistan's sizable Shia minority. The Shias naturally looked to their coreligionists in Iran for support. To a lesser extent Afghanistan's entire Persian-speaking population, which spoke Dari, a variant of the Farsi spoken in

Iran, also hoped for Iran's support. Two decades of civil war had pushed a couple million Afghan refugees into Iran, and the Iranian government was eager to send them home. Iran had also become a main transit route for Afghan opium on its way to Western Europe. Hundreds of Iranian border police and military personnel were killed each year trying to stem this traffic, and significant quantities of the drug found their way into Iranian cities.

From prior experience, I was aware of the role neighboring states often played in fomenting civil wars. Bosnia had been the battleground for Croatian and Serbian ambitions. Likewise, Afghanistan had been the cockpit of Soviet-American competition in the 1980s and the Indo-Pakistani rivalry in the 1990s. I saw little prospect of making an enduring peace among the Afghan factions if their foreign sponsors were not brought into the process.

Burns was not encouraging about the possibilities of my being allowed to work with Tehran. The administration severely limited the contacts he and his staff could undertake. Formally, all communications between the two governments were transmitted through the Swiss embassies in either capital and were supplemented by American and Iranian officials' infrequent meetings under UN auspices in neutral European venues. Those encounters allowed for some modicum of direct communication, but only relatively junior officials spoke and on the basis of heavily circumscribed instructions. As a result, they consisted largely of an exchange of complaints.

Professional diplomats tend to believe that talking with one's adversaries is more productive than not. At best, communication produces accord, and at worst, information. In both Tehran and Washington, however, many influential figures took a distinctly different view. While those who opposed communication argued that it was unlikely to result in agreement, in fact, their main fear was exactly the opposite; that is, communication would indeed lead to mutual accommodation and a gradual improvement of relations. Hard-liners in Iran feared that normal relations with Washington would reduce the revolutionaries' fervor and thereby undermine the legitimacy of their regime, which rested heavily on its anti-American credentials. Conversely, American hard-liners feared normalization would legitimize the regime in Tehran and make its demise less likely.

Burns was not in a position to authorize any contacts on my part with Tehran. For that authorization, he said, I would have to go to Powell, who in turn might need to get a green light from the White House. I decided to bide my time before making any request, preferring to wait until the need for such contacts became more pressing. Both Powell and I were to meet with the Iranians in a larger multilateral setting a few days hence at the United Nations in New York. That contact would suffice for the present.

BEFORE LEAVING Washington I last met with Condoleezza Rice and her deputy, Steve Hadley, in Rice's corner office looking out on the White House lawn. Both greeted me warmly. Hadley and I had collaborated as far back as the Ford administration, during that unique period when Henry Kissinger had been both the national security adviser and the secretary of state. Hadley had worked for Kissinger in the first capacity, and I had in the second. Fifteen years later, Hadley and I had overseen European policy for the Defense and State departments, respectively, and then we had been in almost daily contact. During this latter period we had both encountered Condi Rice, a young Soviet expert on the White House staff. Hadley and Rice had been easy to work with for as long as I had known them. I was confident of their support in the weeks ahead.

We reviewed my mission and proposed plan of action. At this point, I had encountered no interagency policy differences of any consequence, and Hadley and Rice were on board for a UN-sponsored conference to form the next Afghan government. With the ground war in Afghanistan still static, we all assumed that I might have to make several trips to the region to lay the groundwork for the meeting. At this stage there was no practical way for me to get into Afghanistan, so I would have to meet the Afghans in neighboring countries to the north and south. Because no commercial traffic flew over Afghanistan and flying around it could be inordinately time consuming, I said that the State Department would be requesting military airlift to allow me to conduct such shuttle diplomacy. I knew from prior experience that DOD would resist the request and throw the issue to the White House for resolution.

"Don't worry. We'll take care of it," Rice assured me.

BACK AT THE STATE Department I took a secure phone call from Hank Crumpton, the CIA officer overseeing the agency's operations in Afghanistan. Crumpton had been in Afghanistan during my visit to Langley earlier in the week and had told me to call whenever I needed help. He said that Philip Mudd, an agency officer with recent experience on the White House staff, was assigned to accompany me on my forthcoming trip.

In the ten days since taking on the Afghan assignment, I had prepared as best I could. I had learned a little bit more about the country and a good deal more about the considerations and personalities shaping American policy. I was not an Afghanistan expert, but I was more familiar than most people with the difficulties of putting broken countries back together. I did not know much about Central Asia, but I had spent a professional lifetime learning how to marshal and manipulate the instruments of American power, and my advisers were experts in the region. The Bush administration's reservations about nation-building might ultimately present difficulties, but for my mission's current phase I could not have asked for more unqualified support. Indeed, at this stage, the administration, the country, and the entire international community were more unified than in any time in my experience.

4

LAYING THE GROUNDWORK

THE FIRST LEG OF MY JOURNEY took me to New York on November 9, 2001. The UN General Assembly was in the midst of its annual parade of world leaders. This event, normally held in September, had been hurriedly postponed after the attack on the World Trade Center. Even now, more than two months later, security was obtrusive. With President Bush scheduled to make his first appearance before the world body the next day, New York had shut the East River to all maritime traffic, closed airspace over Manhattan, and barred all but official vehicles to the eight lanes of First Avenue in front of the United Nations.

Even after decades of exposure, I found a visit to UN Headquarters exciting. The slim, glass-sheathed Secretariat building rising thirty-nine floors over the East River still looked coolly elegant, even if the interior was beginning to show its age. Next door, the domed chamber of the General Assembly bustled with activity as one great man after another swept in, followed by a train of bag carriers and advisers, for his hour of global exposure. The heads of state and their entourages jostled for space in the elevators and filled the corridors as I made my way past the marbled chamber toward the more modest conference rooms in the basement below, where my own meeting would take place.

Richard Haass and I were in New York for a preliminary gathering of the "Six plus Two" forum, comprising representatives from the six states bordering Afghanistan, plus envoys from the United States, and Russia. Our task

39

was to finalize the text of a communiqué that the eight foreign ministers could issue the following Monday. This joint statement would put their respective governments on record as supporting the UN secretary general's call for all Afghan opposition strands to meet under UN auspices for the purpose of forming a new government. This endorsement would give added weight to UN envoy Lakhdar Brahimi's efforts to convene such a meeting and ensure that whatever emerged from the gathering secured international recognition.

Afghanistan had traditionally been the focal point for competition among its more powerful neighbors. In the nineteenth century, as the Russian and British empires played it, Rudyard Kipling had labeled this geopolitical contest "the great game." As long as regional powers continued to view their competition as a zero-sum contest we saw no prospect of ending the civil war. Securing these governments' backing was thus an essential first step toward any durable reconciliation among the contending Afghan factions.

I HAD FIRST come to the United Nations as a junior diplomat in the early 1970s. It had been an eventful tour of duty, with a Middle East war, an Arab oil embargo, and the Turkish invasion of Cyprus all played out in important ways in these same corridors. Later I had returned to New York regularly to coordinate American and UN activities in Somalia, Haiti, Bosnia, and Kosovo. In the summer of 1999, I had come to alert UN secretary general Kofi Annan that he was about to acquire responsibility for governing Kosovo. Now Washington wanted the United Nations to play the central role in organizing the transition in Afghanistan.

From my earliest days at the United Nations I had found multilateral diplomacy more exciting than work in bilateral embassies. My first Foreign Service posting had been to Paris, where everyone, including the ambassador, had been little more than well-informed observers and articulate messengers. We reported on local developments, delivered démarches on Washington's instruction, and sent back the French response. Occasionally we offered advice, but we never made policy decisions. It was pleasant work done in comfortable circumstances, but its most demanding aspects were social.

In New York, by contrast, even fairly junior officers could become negotiators. While the capitals still wrote the instructions, the missives had to be carried out in a dynamic environment, where the views of more than a hundred other governments had to be accommodated in real time and often against close deadlines. Numerous different committees, each requiring an American representative, might meet at any one time. Many of these gatherings sought to produce common statements of collective policy.

As a result, multilateral diplomacy provided more rapid and continuous feedback than was usually available to those tending a single country relationship. Bilateral ambassadors and their staffs could spend years persuading their host government to take a course of action Washington desired. At the United Nations, by contrast, issues were either decided by consensus or put to a vote every day. The American view might prevail in whole, in part, or not at all. Win, lose, or tie, the scoreboard posted the results each time the ballots were tallied. The issues were sometimes trivial and the results ephemeral, but the sense of success or failure at the end of each workday was nevertheless palpable.

WITH A FAMILIAR tingle of anticipation I made my way through the crowded halls in search of our meeting's venue. The U.S. delegation first had a preliminary exchange with the Russian delegation. It was largely a courtesy, as we had no reason to anticipate difficulties from this quarter. Russian president Vladimir Putin had been the first head of state to call George Bush after 9/11, or at least his was the first call Bush had chosen to take. Subsequently, Washington had been pleasantly surprised to find Putin encouraging the leaders of Uzbekistan and Tajikistan, two former Soviet republics still closely aligned with Moscow, to accede to American requests for overflight rights and basing privileges. For his part, Putin seized on the 9/11 attack as an excuse to wrap Russia's ongoing suppression of the Chechen separatist insurgency in the mantle of Washington's newly declared war on terror. Moscow had long supported the Northern Alliance and happily collaborated with the United States in overthrowing the Taliban. It made sense not to take the Russians' support for granted, however; at some point Moscow's influence might prove decisive. A quick comparison of our notes indicated that the U.S. and Russian objectives for the forthcoming meeting were identical.

As we talked, the other delegations drifted in. Ours was only one of a dozen different meetings on as many various topics taking place in adjoining conference rooms, and several hundred people milled about the hall in search of the right gathering. Haass pointed out to me the senior Iranian representative, a white-haired but rather young-looking deputy foreign minister named Javad Zarif, whose near flawless English betrayed an American education. Once we were all assembled, Brahimi led our session in his usual low-key, businesslike fashion. The UN staff had prepared the draft of a communiqué that the eight foreign ministers intended to issue when they met three days hence. Our purpose was to go over the text, alter it as necessary, and provisionally approve the statement. As with many well-prepared diplomatic encounters, our intent was to ensure that the ministers would need only read their prepared remarks and assent to an already agreed text.

Brahimi's draft contained all the essential ingredients. It called on the various Afghan opposition elements to join in forming a new government and asked the United Nations to assemble them for this purpose. Our discussion was brief and generally positive. The Pakistani and Iranian delegates squabbled over a point of no great importance to the rest of us, their disagreement indicative of the two governments' generally poor relations. Brahimi eventually tired of trying to find wording acceptable to both parties. He asked the two delegations to go off on their own and develop language on which they could both agree, which they were able to do.

With that instruction our gathering came to a close. At one level, it had all been rather prosaic. The upcoming meeting of foreign ministers and representatives would likely be even less eventful. We had moved around a few commas; they would do even less. Yet below the surface, a good deal of work had gone into constructing a text all eight governments could support. The results would justify the time invested in sitting through a couple of well-scripted meetings with predictable outcomes. In a few days, when I began speaking with the Afghan opposition leaders, I would do so not just on Washington's behalf, but with a mandate from all the governments that concerned them. This position would give American diplomacy much greater weight and make it much more difficult for any Afghan opposition element to opt out of the political process that we had begun.

AS EVENING FELL I walked the five blocks to the Waldorf Astoria. The hotel's ornate art deco lobby, extending from Madison to Park Avenue, was as crowded as UN Headquarters and with many of the same people. American officials in New York preparing for President Bush's visit the next day already occupied several floors of the building. Other national delegations were also housed there, although none quite so lavishly. With some difficulty I secured a table at one of the hotel's restaurants. Zalmay Khalilzad, who had come up for Bush's visit, joined me there.

Zal gave me the latest news from Afghanistan. The ground war, hitherto so static, had finally begun moving. Earlier in the day the northern city of Mazar-e-Sharif had fallen to Uzbek and Tajik troops under Generals Dostum and Atta. This victory gave the Northern Alliance control of its first major population center and opened an important new line of communications to the outside world. The military action would next likely shift to Kabul. Khalilzad reported that Washington was still reluctant to give the Northern Alliance a green light to take that city.

For weeks National Security Council principals had debated this prospect. Powell and Tenet had warned that the Northern Alliance forces' seizure of Kabul could antagonize Pakistan, bolster Pashtun support for the Taliban, and lead to a bloodbath in the city. Powell had suggested that the city be turned over to the United Nations or that its liberation wait until a Pashtun resistance force could join in its seizure. Neither alternative struck me as remotely feasible, given that no Pashtun or UN force existed that was capable of assuming or even sharing control of the city. The United States itself had no more than a few dozen soldiers in country at this point. Sometimes, when top officials come together to confront intractable problems, wishful thinking can substitute for realistic analysis. This report had struck me as one of those occasions.

Khalilzad and I agreed that the Northern Alliance was unlikely to wait until the United Nations or the Pashtun resistance, such as it was, could pull together an occupation force for Kabul, particularly since neither was currently doing so. Nor, we thought, did it make sense for the United States to slow the military campaign's pace while awaiting either of these developments.

Even as we discussed the subject, our superiors in Washington fashioned another bureaucratic compromise. They decided that American aircraft would help the Northern Alliance overrun the Taliban defensive lines north of the city but only on the condition that alliance commanders would agree not to send their troops into the capital until UN or Pashtun troops showed up to participate in the occupation.

THE NEXT MORNING, after Bush's speech, I walked back to UN Headquarters, where I met with senior European officials in town for the General Assembly session. The 9/11 attacks had struck a chord throughout the Atlantic world. *Le Monde*, the Paris daily, had run the story under the headline "We Are All Americans!" The NATO Council, for the only time in its fifty-year history, had invoked the article in its charter that defines an attack on any one member as an attack on them all. Thus, the entire NATO alliance had effectively declared war on those responsible for the attacks on New York and Washington. Many allied governments were eager to send troops or planes to Afghanistan and participate in the military campaign.

Washington had deflected most of these offers. Only the United Kingdom played any significant role in the war. The practical reasons that led the administration to rebuff the others' efforts to join the military campaign were real enough. Few allies, the British excepted, had any way of getting their troops or aircraft into the theater without American assistance. Despite massive diplomatic and logistical efforts, the United States itself had not yet succeeded in getting more than a handful of soldiers into Afghanistan. American combat aircraft flew missions from bases or aircraft carriers in the Persian Gulf, the Indian Ocean, and the Bay of Bengal. No European air force could operate from those ranges.

I was less sympathetic to the strain of unilateralist thinking that reinforced these practical considerations. Many in the Bush administration were determined not to repeat the "war by committee" that, in their view, had marred the Kosovo air war two years earlier. Personally, I regarded that campaign as a textbook illustration of the successful use of military force to achieve political purposes at the lowest possible cost. I believed the constraints under which U.S. Air Force generals had then chafed were entirely appropriate, necessary, and efficacious. They had led directly to the NATO victory that an unrestricted air campaign would almost certainly have forgone.

At the same time, I could see that America's allies had less to offer in this latest campaign, and, consequently, we had less reason to share the war's management with them. War by committee made eminent sense when our allies were supplying much of the manpower, equipment, and money. They were not and could not in the Afghan case.

This situation would change, however, once the operation's current phase ended. If Europe's power projection capacity was puny compared to America's, the opposite equation applied in regard to peacekeeping, political reform, and economic development. Where development assistance was concerned, Washington was the dwarf and Europe the giant. In both Bosnia and Kosovo the allies had supplied four-fifths of the peacekeepers and a similar proportion of the economic aid. We could not expect a comparable commitment for far-away Afghanistan, but I did want to lay the groundwork for a more robust allied role once the conventional battle was won.

LATER IN THE MORNING I met with Brahimi for our first private session since I had taken the Afghan assignment. We had coffee in the staff cafeteria that looked out over the East River. He agreed that the United Nations should announce a time and place for a conference rather than wait for the Afghans to agree among themselves on such details. Brahimi did not want to take such a step, however, until reasonably assured that the Afghans' response would be positive. Getting that assurance was my task.

We both expected the Northern Alliance to take Kabul in the near future. The victors would then certainly propose that the meeting to choose the next government should take place in the nation's capital. Allowing the Northern Alliance this home field advantage would be anathema to everyone else. Brahimi recommended, therefore, holding the conference somewhere in Western Europe, perhaps Geneva, where the United Nations had its European headquarters.

He intended to invite delegations from four different opposition factions. The two chief groupings would be the mostly Tajik, Uzbek, and Shia Northern Alliance and the more ethnically balanced supporters of the former king, Zahir Shah. The less consequential third and fourth delegations would be recruited among émigré leaders resident in Pakistan and among opposition figures with links to Iran, respectively. The Pakistani-based faction became known as the Peshawar group, after the border town where many of them lived. The pro-Iranian faction had held several of its meetings in Cyprus, and so we dubbed it the Cyprus group.

None of these factions were homogeneous, nor were their alignments clear cut. The Northern Alliance contained Pashtun elements just as the royalists' group included Tajiks and Uzbeks. Many in the Peshawar faction were critical of Pakistan's policies while the Cyprus group was not all that close to Tehran. Still, by involving these four delegations, Brahimi ensured that most major constituent groups of Afghan society were represented and that all the external powers that had been fueling the Afghan civil war would have at least some sympathetic elements at the meeting.

Brahimi and I disagreed on one significant point: I wanted these neighboring powers invited to participate in the upcoming conference. Brahimi did not. My points of reference were the international processes that had ended the Bosnian and Kosovo conflicts. In both cases the United States, Russia, and the major European powers had coalesced to impose a peace settlement on the warring parties. At the Dayton Accords in 1995 Richard Holbrooke had managed a particularly complex negotiation involving the Muslim, Catholic, and Orthodox factions in Bosnia; their external sponsors in Serbia and Croatia; and the major powers of Western Europe and Russia. Four years later the Kosovo air war had been brought to a close through two parallel negotiations—one involving Russia, the European Union, and Serbia and the other involving the eight major industrial powers, that is, the United States, Japan, Germany, France, Britain, Italy, Canada, and Russia. The first of these two forums had negotiated Serbia's withdrawal from Kosovo while the second had designed the regime that would replace it. Neither the Bosnian nor the Kosovo conflicts could have ended without the active collaboration of these external powers.

Brahimi's model for the upcoming Afghan conference was the peace process he had led ten years earlier that ended the Lebanese civil war. While external actors, including Syria, Israel, and the United States, had all exercised their influence, only the Lebanese parties had been actual participants in those negotiations. For the past several years, Brahimi had been seeking to broker a similar process among the warring Afghan parties, but he had found the regional governments largely unhelpful to his efforts.

Brahimi therefore concluded that reaching a settlement among the

Afghan factions with outside powers participating would be difficult. I countered it would be hard to accomplish without them. We were both right. Whichever path we chose would not be easy.

Brahimi wanted to take the Afghans to an isolated location and sequester them as much as possible from any contact with the outside world, including the particular governments I was proposing to invite. By contrast, I proposed a two-tiered process in which meetings of these foreign governments' representatives would coincide with those of the Afghan parties' delegates.

Brahimi was tough minded and tenacious, but he was also gracious and averse to extended argument. He acknowledged the need for American help in herding the Afghans toward some common outcome. He further recognized that he could not bring the American representative into the process but exclude all the other interested governments. For my part, I was far from sure that the two-ring circus I was proposing was workable. So having aired the pros and cons of our respective positions, we put the issue aside for a while.

MY LAST ENCOUNTER of the weekend took place at the Pakistani mission to the United Nations. There Christina Rocca and Wendy Chamberlin joined me for a meeting with one of President Musharraf's top aides. Musharraf himself had just met with George Bush earlier that day.

Throughout the 1980s Pakistani military intelligence had been the principal channel for covert American support to those Afghan groups resisting the Soviet occupation. This setup had proved a mixed blessing. While providing the United States with an effective conduit for guns and money, it had allowed the Pakistanis to determine who received the aid. The Pakistani Inter-Services Intelligence Directorate had tended to favor the most extreme and fundamentalist mujahideen groups. After the Soviets' withdrawal in 1989, American assistance had ceased. The ISI, however, continued to support the more religiously extreme factions in Afghanistan and from among them fostered the emergence of the Taliban. After 9/11 the American and Pakistani intelligence services found themselves suddenly aligned once again, this time in seeking to overthrow the very regime the ISI had installed in Kabul. Many on the American side now questioned the sincerity of Pakistan's commitment to this new goal.

My Pakistani interlocutor propounded a line of argument I would hear repeatedly in the coming weeks. Pakistan supported ousting the Taliban; however, any replacement government needed to be dominated by the same Pashtun ethnic group because, the Pakistanis argued, the great majority of Afghans were Pashtuns. Further, they maintained Kabul should not be liberated until a Pashtun or international force could take it.

I responded that putting Afghanistan back together was going to be hard as long as its neighbors squabbled over its future. In this connection, I noted, Pakistan seemed badly isolated, as all the other regional governments regarded Pakistani policy with considerable suspicion and were collaborating to oppose it. Reflecting on the previous day's debate between the Pakistani and Iranian representatives over the wording of the Six plus Two group's communiqué, I suggested that perhaps Pakistan should try to improve its relations with these other regional powers, particularly the most important one, Iran. Unless Islamabad and Tehran could overcome their differences, I suggested, promoting the emergence of a stable and representative replacement for the Taliban regime would be more difficult.

It was hard to tell whether my Pakistani or American listeners were more taken aback at my suggestion that seeking rapprochement with Iran might be a good thing. For twenty years successive U.S. administrations had done their best to isolate Iran. My task, however, was a narrow one. Experience convinced me that I was not going to succeed if Afghanistan's two most powerful neighbors remained at loggerheads over the composition of Afghanistan's future government.

LATE IN THE AFTERNOON I flew back to Washington and drove to my home in a quiet, wooded neighborhood where the city blends into its Maryland suburbs. As they did most weekends my two grown sons, Christian and Colin, joined my wife, Toril, and me for a family dinner. The meal ended, as usual, with the two boys good-humoredly disputing whose turn it was to do the dishes.

EARLY MONDAY I returned to UN Headquarters. I found the place buttoned up more than normal with extra guards posted. Knots of people stood around, talking excitedly. Approaching one group, I learned that a plane had dropped out of the sky after taking off from LaGuardia Airport. Moments earlier it had crashed into a residential neighborhood just across the river from us. Everyone immediately assumed it was another terrorist attack. Authorities had already closed all bridges and tunnels into and out of the island of Manhattan and had suspended train and bus service as was all air traffic.

I stood at the entrance to the General Assembly building, wondering what to do next. Would our meeting take place? Would my flight to Europe that evening leave on schedule? How, in any case, would I get to the airport with all the bridges and tunnels closed? Detaching himself from another group, Joschka Fischer, the German foreign minister, approached me. Like everyone he was shaken by the news. We had worked together on Kosovo and Bosnia. He was pleased that I had taken on the Afghan assignment, and we talked a bit about its prospects.

Moments later a motorcade deposited Colin Powell inside a large canvas marquee installed in front of the General Assembly building. Security had raised this tent to deny a sniper perched in some high-rise across First Avenue a line of sight on arriving VIPs. Despite all the excitement, the other foreign ministers also assembled more or less on schedule. The meeting proceeded without incident. In its course, information arrived about casualties from the downed aircraft, which we still assumed was the target of an act of terrorism. Iranian foreign minister Kamal Kharrazi picked up his pen and added a sentence to his prepared remarks in which he declared that Iran stood with the United States against such terrorism and expressed his sorrow at the loss of life. After the minister delivered his statement, an aide took the text with his handwritten addition and brought it to an officer from the American Mission, who then passed it to Powell.

At the meeting's conclusion Powell walked around the room and shook hands and chatted briefly with each of his colleagues, including the Iranian foreign minister. This slight courtesy turned out to be the meeting's most newsworthy moment.

My mission now had all the international backing I could desire. With the bridges, trains, and airports closed, my next challenge would be getting out of town. As the day wore on, however, terror alert levels began to fall after the authorities concluded that the morning's airliner crash had been an accident. The East River bridges were open by the time Powell's motorcade headed out to LaGuardia, where he had a plane waiting to take him back to Washington. I peeled off there and made my way across Long Island to Kennedy Airport. My own flight to Europe left on schedule. The plane was almost empty.

5

ON THE ROAD

ON NOVEMBER 13 THE TEAM SUPPORTING my mission assembled for the first time at the American Embassy in Rome. Craig Karp from the State Department and U.S. Army Col. Jack Gill from the Joint Staff were our area experts. Karp had followed events in Afghanistan for years from various postings in the region, and Gill was a South Asian specialist with more than a decade of experience. Both knew the major Afghan players either personally or by reputation. Bill Luti, a retired naval officer serving as Peter Rodman's deputy in the Office of the Secretary of Defense, and Larry Franklin, a more junior official in that same office, represented the Pentagon's civilian side. As promised, John McLaughlin had assigned an agency officer to the team, Phil Mudd, who would provide us the vital link to Afghan field commanders and political leaders operating inside that country. Accompanying us were several State Department Diplomatic Security Service (DSS) agents whose job was to get us all home safely.

Our main purpose in Rome was to meet with the former king, Zahir Shah, around whom a group of prominent Afghans in exile had formed. First, however, we paid a call at the Italian Foreign Ministry. As hosts to the former king for many years the Italian government had developed considerable insights into the émigré community that surrounded him. Italian diplomats advocated a major role for him and his faction in determining Afghanistan's future. During our discussions, the Italians stressed that some sort of peace-keeping mission would be needed in Afghanistan, and they tentatively offered to contribute a contingent of police.

Following our meeting at the Foreign Ministry we encountered the first setback of the trip. I had intended to fly from Rome to either Uzbekistan or Tajikistan and meet with the Northern Alliance's political leadership. If I could get both the king and the Northern Alliance to send representatives to Brahimi's meeting, all the other invitees would surely fall in line. After checking with his colleagues in Afghanistan, however, Phil Mudd reported that all the leading Northern Alliance political and military figures were in country and unavailable for meetings in any of the neighboring capitals. Several weeks earlier Foreign Minister Abdullah had offered to come to Washington to consult, but the administration, not yet ready to talk seriously, had declined. Now we were eager for a meeting, and the Northern Alliance, it seemed, was not.

This development portended what I had feared most, long days spent cooling our heels in distant hotel rooms while waiting for someone worth talking with to appear. While not exactly a hardship, it would be a waste of time and energy. We heard the bad news while lunching on the upper deck of a barge tied to the bank of the Tiber River, which flows through central Rome. Our view and our food were spectacular, but we soon became so preoccupied in rerouting our mission that we had scant time to notice either. Each of us had a cell phone, and our embassy escorts lent us a couple more. Some of us conducted two calls at once, which precluded our eating. At one point, as the main course was being served, we had seven conversations going simultaneously with our embassies in Tashkent, Dushanbe, and Islamabad; the State and Defense departments; CENTCOM; and the CIA. Other diners looked askance at the table of American boors who did not have the courtesy to talk to each other, let alone give their meal the attention it deserved.

By the time coffee was served, we had succeeded in reorganizing our travel. We would leave the next day for Turkey and then to Pakistan, where we would meet with representatives of the large Afghan refugee community. This activity would keep us usefully employed for a few days.

A year or two earlier I had read a magazine article describing a long weekend in Richard Holbrooke's Balkan shuttle diplomacy. Holbrooke had had a plane, a negotiating team, and a reporter in tow but no clear plan. Key interlocutors were unavailable, rendezvous fell through, meetings produced little, and several days of jetting around the Balkans seemed to yield few results. Defending his peripatetic approach, Holbrooke had explained to the accompanying journalist that diplomacy was really more like jazz than classical music, meaning it required a great deal of improvisation. At the time I thought he provided a clever rationalization for a largely lost weekend. Now, having myself assembled a delegation, wrangled an airplane, secured international backing, and created some expectation of success, I was inclined to view his musical analogy more tolerantly.

We learned that while we had been crossing the Atlantic, the White House had announced that the Northern Alliance leadership had promised President Bush that its forces would not enter Kabul until UN or Pashtun forces were ready to join them. Having secured this pledge, the president unleashed American aircraft to begin pounding the capital's outer defenses. Rather than falling back and fighting house to house, however, reports indicated that the Taliban was abandoning the city altogether. I wondered why the president's credibility had been staked upon such an improbable promise.

That evening we drove out to the Roman suburbs for a call on the old Afghan king. The Italian authorities gave us a police escort, I thought more as a gesture of solidarity than out of any real concern for our safety. As our motorcade zoomed through rush-hour traffic, sirens wailing, one of our cars clipped the side mirror off another vehicle. The irate Italian motorist pursued us for several miles, honking fruitlessly and shaking his fist.

The former king lived in a gated community of upper-middle-class homes. Described as a villa, the house was comparatively modern, rather unpretentious, and distinguishable from its neighbors chiefly by the squad of Italian Carabinieri guarding its perimeter. Zahir greeted us warmly and invited us to take seats around the coffee table in his living room. At eighty-seven years old, he looked his age and spoke in quiet, almost hesitant tones. He stressed his desire to facilitate the formation of a broadly based, representative government in Afghanistan. He promised willingly that his supporters would participate in the conference Brahimi intended to call. They were ready to work with all other elements of the opposition, including the Northern Alliance.

Zahir struck me as mentally alert but physically frail. He did not impress me as having a particularly forceful or decisive personality. He was prepared to lend his name and prestige to the process of constituting a new

Afghan government, but he said that he sought no formal role for himself. Some of his entourage, I had been warned, had other ideas.

As we prepared to leave, several of these individuals introduced themselves, including the king's grandson, Mustafa. This ebullient young man spoke enthusiastically of the resistance movement that was spreading throughout Afghanistan's Pashtun south. He and his colleagues in Rome had contacts with numerous bands of resistance fighters. Their rallying cry, he said, was a call for convening a *loya jirga*, or grand council, at which a new government would be named.

Since the Northern Alliance already had a government and seemed about to reoccupy the capital, this appeal was clearly designed to challenge that regime's legitimacy. I did not doubt that many tribal leaders in Afghanistan's Pashtun-dominated south and west were hedging their bets and contacting Zahir's entourage in a search for new patrons; however, as yet, we saw little sign of organized resistance in this community.

As we took our leave the king, a frangible but lucid figure, enjoyed a cigar and joked with members of my team. Returning to Rome, again through the evening rush hour, our police escort cleared all three lanes of the *autostrada*, avoiding any further incidents but antagonizing even more rush-hour commuters.

Back downtown, we found a restaurant near our hotel. Our conversation naturally turned to the task before us and to the prospective part I envisaged for Afghanistan's neighbors in helping us put together a new government. At the mention of Iran, Bill Luti, hitherto relaxed and genial, became agitated. He vehemently said that he found the idea of engaging Iran, for any purpose, anathema. I countered that we would not be able to reconcile the various Afghan factions if their foreign sponsors were giving them conflicting advice. As the discussion progressed, Luti's voice rose to the point where other patrons began regarding our table with alarm. For the second time that day we made a spectacle of ourselves.

Perceiving that dispassionate or even discreet discussion on this subject to be impossible, I changed the topic, and Luti reverted to his usual good humor. He said he would return to Washington the following morning and leave his colleague, Larry Franklin, to represent Rumsfeld's civilian staff.

THE NEXT DAY, at the crack of dawn, we flew to Ankara on a small U.S. Air Force Learjet, just large enough to fit everyone. On landing we went to the Foreign Ministry and met with a group of civilian and military officials. Ankara had long-standing connections with elements of the Northern Alliance and in particular with the Uzbek warlord Abdul Rashid Dostum. General Dostum had taken refuge in Turkey during the late 1990s and had only recently returned to Afghanistan. A few days prior to our arrival, Turkish president Ahmed Sezer had met with Burhanuddin Rabbani. Pakistani president Musharraf had also recently visited Ankara. The Turks shared with us the results of their conversations. First, they cautioned against holding Brahimi's upcoming meeting in any country that had recognized the Taliban government. Then they suggested that Hamid Karzai might be a good candidate to head the new Afghan government. The Turks were the first of many to raise this possibility with me.

Arriving back at the airport, we found that the U.S. Air Force had switched our tiny Learjet for a C-17, a massive aircraft capable of accommodating M1 Abrams tanks. Our home for the remainder of the mission was not exactly cozy. Certainly spacious, the plane afforded adequate room to stretch our legs, jog, or play volleyball, if desired, but the accommodations were otherwise remarkably Spartan. Two rows of narrow, upright, non-reclining chairs, of the sort normally found on short-hop commuter flights, had been bolted to the floor. The fuselage was not insulated for sound. Once we were in flight, the noise precluded conversation and the seats, sleep.

The air force had assigned us the C-17 because the more comfortably appointed and appropriately sized jet transports that customarily shuttled generals, congressmen, and other VIPs were unequipped to fly into a war zone; that is, they lacked countermeasures designed to defeat incoming antiaircraft missiles. Our route took us through the Caucasus, Turkmenistan, Uzbekistan, and then over Afghanistan itself. The Taliban did not have an air force, and we were flying well above the range of any antiaircraft weapons they might possess. Still, it was nice to know that the air force had given us the most survivable transport aircraft available.

WE ARRIVED in Islamabad late that evening and were immediately driven to the American Embassy. Here U.S. officials worked and most also lived within a walled, heavily guarded enclave. Craig Karp and I went to the ambassador's residence while the other team members were distributed among several embassy apartments on and off the compound. Embassy spouses and children had been evacuated to the States immediately after 9/11, so there was more room to accommodate visitors than usual. In my case, I occupied the bedroom of Wendy Chamberlin's daughter.

Even as we flew over Afghanistan, Northern Alliance troops had been entering Kabul. Thus I spent much of the following day doing my best to moderate Pakistani chagrin at this development. We met first with the foreign secretary, Inam ul-Haq, and then with Aziz Ahmed Khan, the deputy foreign minister. Later in the day we met with Lt. Gen. Ehsan ul-Haq, the head of Inter-Services Intelligence. The general was the son of the former military dictator, Zia ul-Haq, who, along with the then American ambassador, had been killed in a mysterious plane crash in 1988.

It had largely been at Pakistan's behest that President Bush had pressed the Northern Alliance leadership not to enter Kabul until a UN or Pashtun force could be organized to assist in the occupation. Pakistani officials conveyed to me repeatedly and at length their unhappiness at the Northern Alliance's violation of its pledge. The Pakistanis professed to fear the prospect of undisciplined Northern Alliance troops waging reprisals and looting. They warned that Pashtun militias would organize to resist the occupation and contest control of the city, occasioning large-scale destruction and loss of life. As both these things had happened in the past decade, these fears were not unreasonable. The most pressing Pakistani concern, however, went unstated: any Northern Alliance-dominated government would be beholden to India, which had supported its resistance to the Taliban, and would therefore be hostile to Pakistan, which had backed the losing side. Pakistan would consequently find itself encircled by unfriendly neighbors: India to the south, Iran to the west, and Afghanistan to the north.

Pakistani officials insisted that Pashtuns would need to dominate any representative Afghan government. This view represented more than Pakistani dedication to democratic principles. Since more Pashtuns lived in Pakistan than in Afghanistan, and since communications across the long, rugged frontier between the two countries were largely unregulated, any Pashtun-dominated government would be susceptible to Pakistani influence. The ethnically based principle upon which this claim to Pashtun preeminence was based was debatable, and the demographics equally so, given the uncertainty about the actual strength of Afghanistan's various communities. The geopolitical message was clear enough, though: Pakistan was going to be hostile to any Afghan government it could not influence.

That Pashtuns had dominated Afghan governments since the country's emergence as a nation state in the eighteenth century was irrefutable, and clearly Pakistan was determined that they should continue to do so. The United States, for its part, wanted the Taliban to be excluded from the next Afghan government. The problem, therefore, was to identify Pashtun leaders who could speak for their community but who were not compromised by their complicity with the prior regime. There were not many, thanks in part to the successful Pakistani efforts over the past twenty years in marginalizing moderate voices.

I could only do so much to assuage Pakistani concerns. They had backed the losing horse and could not expect to immediately switch to a winner. Neither Washington nor the Northern Alliance leadership would allow the Taliban into the new government, and as yet no Pashtun resistance movement of any consequence existed. American forces were not going to wrest Kabul or other major population centers from Northern Alliance control. The best I could do was listen, express sympathy, urge patience, and promise that the United States would use its considerable influence to ensure that the next Afghan government was broadly representative and had substantial Pashtun participation.

Whereas the foreign secretary had mostly just complained, ISI director Haq had a constructive suggestion to make. He proposed that Hamid Karzai might be an acceptable choice to head the next Afghan government. Haq was the second person in as many days to suggest a Karzai candidacy. I assumed he knew that the CIA had been assisting Karzai in gathering a band of resistance fighters. Haq's suggestion therefore might be read as an effort to find common ground with Washington. I responded noncommittally, as I had no idea whether Karzai would prove tolerable to the other factions. Still, I was intrigued at how his name kept cropping up.

OVER DINNER that evening I met with the Pakistani journalist Ahmed Rashid. In a stroke of perfect timing, his recently published account of the rise of the Taliban had become a worldwide best-seller. He warned me that disentangling this fundamentalist Afghan movement from its Pakistani sponsors would prove difficult.

THE FOLLOWING morning we clambered aboard our jumbo craft for a short flight to Peshawar, capital of Pakistan's North-West Frontier Province. This land was Rudyard Kipling country, where for centuries the hawk-nosed Pathans (the British term for Pashtuns) had been slipping back and forth through the nearby Khyber Pass that links Pakistan and Afghanistan. In recent years the city and its surrounding region had become home to several million Afghan refugees.

We spent much of the next twenty-four hours on the screened veranda of our consul-general's residence meeting with assorted local Afghan leaders. Their uniform message was that the Northern Alliance's entry into Kabul was a catastrophe. They wanted an international peacekeeping force dispatched to that city immediately and felt that Zahir Shah was the only rallying point for all Afghans.

We had two particularly memorable encounters there. One was with several representatives of Afghan women. Their aspirations for relief from harsh Taliban repression, for secure access to education and health care, and for participation in the political process for their fellow women were couched in moderate terms. Afghanistan was a conservative society, and these women's expectations for change were realistically gradualist.

Our second encounter was less agreeable. It was with James Ritchie, one of two wealthy American brothers who had moved to Peshawar in the hopes of joining the "great game." After 9/11 the Ritchies had pursued a long-standing interest in promoting regime change in Afghanistan and backed their own guerrilla force. Their first venture had gone badly awry. They had bankrolled Abdul Haq's ill-fated foray across the border several weeks earlier, although local CIA officers had counseled Haq against the enterprise and deprecated the Ritchie brothers' amateurish efforts. The consulate asked me to meet with James, who had remained in Peshawar and still wanted to be involved in overthrowing the Taliban.

Ritchie said that he and his brother wished to support the emergence of a democratic Afghanistan. I responded that funding insurgents was not the best way for private citizens to help. I suggested that he and his brother might better direct their efforts and money to supporting the growth of Afghan civil society once a new regime had been put in place. In this connection, I cited the work the American philanthropist George Soros and the Open Society Foundation had done in the Balkans. Ritchie was clearly more interested in armed insurrection than in civil society. He went away visibly unhappy.

That evening we called on the governor of the North-West Frontier Province, Syed Iftikhar Hussain Shah. His official residence was an enormous version of a British colonial bungalow, original parts of which actually dated back to the Raj. In the 1970s a Pakistani government still imbued with imperial tradition added other wings. We entered a garden impressively lit with hundreds of flaming torches and were offered tea on the veranda. In his assessment of the Afghan situation the governor was alarmist and characterized it as a "doomsday scenario" for Pakistan. Taliban supporters were deeply entrenched within the Pakistan border regions, he warned, where they were numerous and well organized. He seemed quite pessimistic about Pakistan's ability to control this population.

THE FOLLOWING MORNING we went to see Rustam Shah Momand, a Pakistani diplomat who had negotiated on Islamabad's behalf with the Northern Alliance some years earlier. He had since apparently fallen out of favor, perhaps because of that association, for he now occupied a rather obscure post in the local provincial administration. His views on the situation in Kabul and the prospects for working with the Northern Alliance were balanced and thoughtful. He urged us to work with the Northern Alliance leadership to form a new government and said that we should hold the upcoming conference in Kabul, if necessary. If we failed to rapidly seize the opportunity opened by the Taliban's collapse, he stressed, Afghanistan could plunge into yet another civil war. Some months later I was pleased to see President Musharraf appoint Momand as his first post-Taliban ambassador to Kabul.

FLYING BACK to Islamabad that afternoon, we returned to the American Embassy compound. Pending the availability of Northern Alliance representatives, we had little to do. I had met in New York or on the road with representatives of all the governments that could influence events in Afghanistan and with all the main opposition factions except the Northern Alliance.

Washington was, nevertheless, becoming impatient. The military campaign was accelerating rapidly, and the Taliban's total collapse seemed imminent. Yet nothing seemed to be happening on the diplomatic front.

Christina Rocca called. "The secretary wants you to go to Kabul."

"Fine. Can our military provide the transport and security?" I asked.

"Don't know," she replied. "I'll get back to you."

Shortly thereafter, Gen. Tommy Franks called to relay the same message. "Washington wants you to go to Kabul," he reported.

"Can you make the necessary logistic and security arrangements?" I asked.

"Oh, I think you will be safe enough," Franks replied evasively.

I took his reply as a negative answer. Franks had no one in Kabul and thus no way to arrange a visit. The State Department could do even less to help.

I sensed that Washington was in a "don't just stand there, do something" mode. My mission seemed to have run out of steam, leaving us stranded in Islamabad with no one worth talking to and nothing useful to do. The war was close to being won, but peace seemed as distant as ever.

About this same time the White House contacted Brahimi in New York and asked that he drop his insistence that the conference of opposition figures take place on neutral ground outside Afghanistan. The White House suggested instead that the meeting be held at Bagram Air Base. Brahimi thought the proposal was both undesirable and impractical. He declined to consider it.

The CIA finally broke the logjam. Since we had left Washington, Gary Berntsen, the clandestine service officer at General Fahim's headquarters, had been pressing the Northern Alliance political leadership to contact me. Fahim and Foreign Minister Abdullah had made excuses, leading Berntsen to conclude that perhaps Fahim wanted to send someone other than Abdullah. Finally Berntsen convinced Abdullah to meet us, and he arranged to fly Abdullah out of the country. Mudd reported that the foreign minister would be available to see me the following day in Tashkent.

EARLY THE NEXT MORNINg we were back aboard our big bird for another flight over the Hindu Kush. This time the pilot invited me up front to enjoy the scenery. The view was stunning. Unlike the rest of the aircraft, the cockpit was well insulated, and we could converse in an almost normal tone of voice. The windows were extremely large, extending from the ceiling to the floor. With the sudden silence and panoramic view, it was almost as if we were appended to a balloon as we flew over the knife-edged, snow-capped peaks below and crossed the Wahkan Corridor, that narrow strip of Afghanistan that extends all the way to the Chinese border.

On arriving in Tashkent the American ambassador, John Herbst, met us at the airport. Once again, I felt rather foolish as our small party debarked from the immense aircraft. Herbst drove us directly to his home, where we were to meet Abdullah. On the way from the airport, I looked around and was greatly disappointed. Tashkent, like Samarkand and Bukhara, evoked the storied East and caravan routes and nomadic tribesmen. Unfortunately, the city bore no visible trace of its exotic past. Under a hazy winter sky we drove past one shoddy, run-down apartment block after another, the legacy of Soviet urban planning compounded by an earthquake that had leveled most of the city's historic buildings in 1966.

The ambassador's residence was a modest but comfortable house built around a small courtyard. After the Soviet Union collapsed a decade earlier, the State Department had suddenly needed to establish more than a dozen new embassies in the newly independent republics. Done on a shoestring budget, the new missions were not the stately homes and palatial chancelleries that mark the American presence in established capitals. Still, we had been up since well before dawn and had flown across the roof of the world, so we were grateful for the ambassador's warm and collegial welcome.

Shortly after our arrival Gary Berntsen was shown in. Wearing a turtleneck pullover, bomber jacket, and boots, the unshaven Berntsen was the image of an action hero. Intense and highly charged, he was eager to help us in any way he could. Just before leaving Kabul and bringing Abdullah to us, he had spoken by satellite phone with his boss, Hank Crumpton, at CIA headquarters.

"Treat Dobbins as you would the director," Crumpton had instructed. "Tell him everything about the agency's activities in Afghanistan in as much detail as possible. Hold nothing back." Crumpton had also directed Berntsen to take us with him to Afghanistan if we chose, to house us with his team, and to ensure our security. I had worked with agency personnel on and off for more than thirty years and had never encountered an embrace quite like this one.

Berntsen assured me that the capital was quiet. Northern Alliance troops had occupied Kabul without incident.

"Tell me about Abdullah," I said.

"He is a serious person and influential within the Northern Alliance hierarchy."

"Can I trust him?"

"You can trust him to pursue the Northern Alliance's interests," Berntsen replied. He also cautioned that Abdullah had threatened to resign a couple of days earlier over the British troops' unannounced arrival at Bagram Air Base. He was still quite upset over the incident.

I declined Berntsen's offer to relocate to Kabul with him, noting that my immediate priority was to get the Northern Alliance to attend the UN-sponsored conference, which would probably take place somewhere in Europe. I thanked him for delivering Abdullah and expressed admiration for the work that he, his agency, and his Special Forces colleagues had done over the past several weeks. As we were speaking, we were alerted that Abdullah had arrived and was being shown to an adjoining sitting room. A few moments later we joined him there.

After briefly exchanging pleasantries, Abdullah came right to the point. The Northern Alliance leaders were grateful for American assistance. They regretted having had to enter Kabul earlier than anticipated, but they could not afford to leave the city unsecured once the Taliban withdrew. They understood the need to form a broadly based government and were prepared to work with the United Nations and other Afghan opposition elements in order to do so. They preferred that a meeting to this end take place in Kabul, but they would consider other locations. Finally, they did not think it fair that the Northern Alliance should participate in this meeting as one of four delegations. The royalists they could accept as more or less equal negotiating partners, but they felt the other two groups Brahimi proposed to invite were not of comparable importance.

We spent some time going over each of these issues. Abdullah was organized and businesslike. He spoke an accented but precise English. When pressed on the matters he had raised, he responded clearly and constructively. The

Northern Alliance would not insist on Kabul as the site for Brahimi's meeting. It would bargain hard about its level of participation to keep from becoming an artificially constructed minority, but it would not allow that matter to become an obstacle for holding the meeting.

For my part, I assured Abdullah that the United States would actively work with the United Nations to ensure the success of its conference. That the Northern Alliance was one of four groups to be represented did not imply that we thought all four had equal weight. We would take decisions by consensus, not balloting, so the alliance faced no danger of being outvoted. Moreover, participation in the new government would not be proportional to each faction's participation in the conference. The United States and the rest of the international community understood the essential role the Northern Alliance had played in opposing and ultimately defeating the Taliban.

As Berntsen had warned, Abdullah then registered the alliance's unhappiness with the British troops' uncoordinated appearance at Bagram several days earlier. He noted that all the American deployments to Afghanistan had been closely coordinated with the Northern Alliance leadership, and he demanded to know why the British had not done the same. I said it had been an oversight, not a calculated gesture, and reassured him it would not happen again. In truth, I had no information on the incident beyond what I had read in the press. I certainly had no authority to speak for Her Majesty's Government, but this line seemed the right one to take. I thought British authorities were unlikely to make the same mistake twice.

Abdullah proposed that I return with him to Afghanistan the next day and meet the rest of the Northern Alliance leadership. Instead of going to Kabul, he said the members would travel to Bagram to meet with my team and me. I readily agreed. I knew this trip would please my superiors in Washington, who were eager for progress on the political front and keen to register a visible American diplomatic presence in country.

I suggested to Abdullah that before leaving Tashkent we should hold a joint press conference. It would help me lock in the commitments that Abdullah had made and ensure against any slippage that my discussions with the larger group of Northern Alliance leaders the next day might occasion. Abdullah readily agreed. We arranged to meet again later in the day for that purpose.

FROM HERBST'S HOUSE our team went to a brand-new InterContinental Hotel, where we would be spending the night. The contrast between this plush, supermodern exemplar of five-star hostelry and the surrounding city could not have been starker. Inside, one could easily have been in Manhattan, London, or Tokyo. The staff wore nicely tailored uniforms while the guests sported stylish designer jeans or business suits. Outside, all was worn, shoddy, and unfashionable. Taking a short stroll late in the afternoon, I felt distinctly uncomfortable walking across the edge of the hotel's beautifully kept grounds into the drab, down-at-the-heels world around it.

THE AFTERNOON'S PRESS conference went well. Abdullah repeated the assurances he had given me earlier in the day. We both spent time trying to tamp down stories of a major rift between Great Britain and the Northern Alliance over the former's unannounced descent on Bagram Air Base.

It was late by the time I had filed my reports to Washington and returned to the hotel for dinner with some team members. The only place still open was a Mexican restaurant in the basement. The decor was Euro-disco with garish colors—pink, purple, lemon yellow. The south-of-the-border ambiance, such as it was, consisted of movie posters from old American Westerns. One featured Alan Ladd in *Shane*. We had burritos and Heinekens and then went to bed.

THE FOLLOWING DAY'S meeting in Bagram solidified the Northern Alliance's promise to attend Brahimi's conference. With the former king's faction and current occupants of Kabul now committed to showing up, I had little doubt that Brahimi would be able to assemble the necessary cast for the next act in our drama.

Leaving Bagram late that afternoon, we took the CIA L-100 aircraft back to Tashkent, where we reboarded our C-17 and flew over Afghanistan for the fourth time in two days. We landed quite late that evening in Islamabad. Despite the hour, Jack Gill and I visited Deputy Foreign Minister Aziz Ahmed Khan at his home. I wanted to give the Pakistanis a firsthand account of my conversations in Tashkent and Bagram before I headed back to Washington. Khan received us in his living room, which was filled with lovely Afghan antiquities from an early posting in Kabul. We then returned to Ambassador Chamberlin's residence, where we sat up much of the night trying to plot an itinerary that could get us back to Washington in time for Thanksgiving.

Early the next morning we boarded our C-17 once again. This time I came prepared, carrying a tattered mattress and sleeping bag that Wendy Chamberlin had donated. With the addition of ear plugs and a sleep mask, I spent much of the next day sleeping on the steel floor. That evening, we landed in London in time for dinner.

The next morning we met with British Foreign Office and Defense Ministry officials. We laid to rest any lingering rifts over the Bagram episode and began planning for the upcoming UN conference, which I learned Brahimi had decided to hold in Bonn. Later that afternoon, we flew to Washington.

6

A SMALL TOWN IN GERMANY

WHEN I FIRST BEGAN TO VISIT the West German capital, it was still the small, quaint, comfortable center of intrigue and power memorialized in John le Carré's classic novel of Cold War espionage, *A Small Town in Germany*. No place on earth had a higher concentration of spies, diplomats, and politicians, at least on weekdays. On weekends the politicians returned to their constituencies, leaving the spies and diplomats free to enjoy the area's idyllic landscape and cozy country inns. It was a great place to raise a young family.

In the mid-1980s I therefore leaped at the opportunity to fill the number two position in the American Embassy. With outposts in a dozen other West German cities, including West Berlin, Bonn was America's largest and arguably most important diplomatic mission. Yet it was also situated in Europe's smallest and most comfortable capital. Professionally, it was the epicenter of European and East-West diplomacy. Privately, it was a quiet university town, situated in the midst of riverside vineyards and rolling hills, many of which were capped with romantic medieval ruins.

By the time I took up residence there, the Cold War was winding down; however, this situation was by no means apparent to those of us living through it. Germany and Europe were still divided and seemed destined to remain so indefinitely. Berlin was still under four-power occupation, with an ugly wall running through its center, and the United States and the Soviet Union still traded spies on the city's scenic Glienicker Bridge. Several hundred thousand American troops still defended West Germany while an equally large number of Russians were still garrisoned in the German Democratic Republic. The Baader-Meinhof gang kept assassinating American and German officials, although Andreas Baader and Ulrike Meinhof were both long dead. The United States still deployed missiles aimed at Moscow as thousands of Germans protested. Travel to Berlin still preceded through narrow air, rail, and road corridors established forty years earlier.

One of my tasks during those years had been to locate a scenic spot from which President Ronald Reagan could address the people of Berlin. Among several possibilities our local mission suggested, I favored a site directly facing the Berlin Wall. I persuaded my ambassador and the White House advance team to ignore the reservations of fainter hearts that thought the location a trifle provocative. On June 12, 1987, only a stone's throw from the Brandenburg Gate, President Reagan issued his appeal: "Mr. Gorbachev, tear down this wall." He used stirring rhetoric, we all thought, with zero chance of getting a positive response.

Two years later I was back in Washington and in temporary charge of the State Department's European Bureau. On a brisk, sunny Saturday morning my secretary put her head into my office.

"President Bush is on the phone. He wants to speak to you," she said, excitedly.

I knew why. Earlier in the day the East German authorities had thrown open all gates in the wall between East and West Berlin. Then-president George H. W. Bush wanted an update on the fast-moving situation there. Thousands of people were streaming back and forth, and all the verities of Cold War geopolitics had gone out the window. Having just returned from a four-year stint in Bonn, I was the only senior official in Washington with any recent German experience. This qualified me to join the small group working with Secretary of State Jim Baker on the whirlwind diplomatic campaign that reunified Germany, ended the Cold War, lifted the Iron Curtain, and healed the nearly half-century-old division of Europe.

Seen from a twenty-first-century perspective, these events appear inevitable, but we did not sense that at the time. Watching President Bush, National Security Adviser Brent Scowcroft, and Secretary Baker guide American diplomacy through these months provided convincing evidence that great statesmen, like great athletes, can make the apparently impossible look easy.

Among the many changes then set in train was the transfer of Germany's capital. By 1999 all the politicians, ministers, officials, diplomats, and spies had decamped to the reunified Berlin. Bonn became a quiet university town again. As such it provided an ideal spot in which to sequester the Afghan opposition parties until they could produce a new government.

AMONG THE FACILITIES left behind when the German government moved to Berlin was a large official guest house. The Petersberg sat atop a heavily wooded hill overlooking the Rhine. From this site, fifty years earlier, the three occupying powers—France, Britain, and the United States—had overseen the birth of the German Federal Republic. By the mid 1950s the Allied High Commission building was deserted, after the American, British, and French governments each opened separate embassies across the river in the suburb of Bad Godesberg. For many years thereafter the hilltop structure had stood largely vacant. Only in the late 1980s did the German government launch a major renovation, designed to turn the site into a guest house capable of accommodating state visitors and their entire retinues. As with many such projects, it went way over budget and beyond schedule and was completed only after most German officials had departed for Berlin.

The German government, eager to put this white elephant to good use, operated the facility as a major international conference center. Among other meetings, the negotiations to end the war in Kosovo had taken place here in 1999. Now Joschka Fischer offered Brahimi this capacious and isolated location in which to seclude his Afghan delegates and allow them to confer in considerable comfort far from the prying eyes of the press or public.

I had already visited the Petersberg many times. It had been visible from my home's terrace in the late 1980s. The building stood at the summit of a symmetrical, heavily wooded hill, reachable only by a single narrow road that wound its way to the top through a dense pine forest. On pleasant fall and spring afternoons I had hiked the trails that threaded its slopes and was rewarded on achieving the crest with an expansive view of the river valley below. I could watch ferries slipping back and forth and heavily laden barges moving slowly upstream and downstream. Several nearby hills were topped with medieval ruins, including the remains of a castle where the German folk hero Siegfried was said to have slain a dragon.

In the summer of 1999, eight delegations had gathered at the Petersberg to work out the terms by which Kosovo would be emptied of Serb troops, occupied by NATO soldiers, and governed by UN administrators. That congress of great powers included the United States, Russia, Britain, France, Italy, and Germany, very much in the nineteenth-century tradition. No Kosovars or Serbs had been invited. I had headed the American delegation to that conference until its concluding days, when Madeleine Albright joined me. Brahimi's meeting would be very different, with the Afghans at its core and the great powers on the periphery. The United States would still have considerable influence over the outcome but would have to exercise it discreetly.

The arrangements for the conference represented a compromise between Brahimi's preference for strictly isolating the Afghans and mine for allowing the key governments' full participation. Representatives of Afghanistan's neighboring states would have access to the site and thus to the Afghans, as I had suggested. Only the Afghans would be permitted to attend the actual negotiating sessions, however, which would take place under Brahimi's chairmanship. No other outsiders would be present.

During the 1999 talks on Kosovo the American Embassy had still been located in Bonn, so I had been able to rely on that facility for office space, staff support, and classified communications. Because all foreign missions had since moved to Berlin, along with most of the German government's offices, this time we would have to establish our own base of operations, a place where our delegation could meet, work, and communicate with our government. For my team, only two or three Americans would be able to find accommodations in the Petersberg itself, as most of the space there was reserved for the Afghans. I therefore took a large block of rooms at a hotel a mile away in the little riverside town of Königswinter, where my team would live and work.

THE GROUP THAT had accompanied me to Bagram had been supplemented by reinforcements from Washington and from several of our diplomatic posts. Christina Rocca lent me her senior adviser on Afghanistan, Jeff Lunstead, who functioned ably as my chief of staff throughout the conference. Condi Rice sent Zal Khalilzad, and Bill Luti reappeared along with Harold Rohde, another Defense Department staffer. The embassy officers who had arranged our visits in Rome and Peshawar also joined us, as they knew many of the Afghan leaders who resided there and who were now gathering in Bonn.

Most of the team members were career professionals who could be expected to provide advice when asked and take direction when given. Luti and Khalilzad, however, were political appointees and representatives of the new administration, not of the permanent bureaucracy. While I worried that they might be inclined to freelance, I recognized they both represented important constituencies that would have to be brought along if Washington was going to buy whatever agreement we could negotiate.

I ARRIVED IN Bonn forty-eight hours ahead of the conference's opening to see to organizational and administrative matters and to become acquainted with as many of the other participants as possible, starting with our hosts. I knew quite a few German diplomats, and I was well known to them. The senior German organizing this conference was Thomas Matussek. We had become acquainted when he was serving as the principal aide to Hans-Dietrich Genscher, the long-serving foreign minister under Chancellor Helmut Kohl. A big bear of a man, with a bluff, hearty demeanor, Matussek was ready to do whatever he could to make this meeting a success. I had little difficulty persuading him that that meant giving a considerable number of American diplomats access to the site and to the Afghan delegates gathered there. Appearances required that all national delegations be treated equally, but Matussek and Brahimi understood that as a result of the ongoing military campaign in Afghanistan, the American representatives were likely to carry the most weight. Since German, American, and UN objectives for this meeting were identical, it made sense for the hosts to accommodate my request for such access.

It was also important, however, that the American hand not be unduly conspicuous, in order to preserve the essential Afghan nature of this gathering and to prevent other national delegations from taking exception to a disproportionately large American presence. Accordingly, I instructed my staff that when visiting the conference site, they should not spend their time chatting together.

"If you can't find an Afghan to talk to, take a walk in the surrounding park. Don't hang about in large groups, making yourselves conspicuous," I urged.

Matussek and I lunched together at an older riverside hotel that Adolf Hitler had reportedly favored. Across the Rhine we could see the conference site perched on its hilltop. During our meal Joschka Fischer called Matussek and expressed his concerns about several German relief workers who were caught in a firefight somewhere in Afghanistan. Learning from Matussek that we were together, Fischer asked to speak to me. Could I secure U.S. help in extricating his endangered compatriots? Before dessert arrived, I had been able to contact the State Department's round-the-clock Operations Center, which in turn put me through to the Pentagon's equivalent, the National Command Center. Its personnel assured me that the Germans were all out of danger.

WHILE WAITING for the Afghans to assemble, I sought out the other national representatives congregating for the conference, particularly the Pakistani, Russian, Indian, and Iranian delegates. Since 1979, their governments had been fighting a proxy war in Afghanistan, with Pakistan supporting the Taliban and the other three opposing it. Should these governments choose to continue their competition, nothing of enduring value would likely be achieved here in Bonn.

India sent a distinguished senior diplomat who had been brought out of retirement for the purpose. White-haired, elegant, soft-spoken, with an English diction I could only envy, Ambassador S. K. Lambha had earlier served in the most demanding of New Delhi's diplomatic postings, as the Indian envoy to Pakistan. Lambha explained to me his government's long-standing ties to the Northern Alliance leadership. He was ready to draw on these relationships to ensure the success of the upcoming conference. I knew that India's interest in Afghanistan stemmed largely from its competition with Pakistan. Lambha understood, however, that the United States needed Islamabad's support to prosecute the war in Afghanistan and was careful not to adopt an anti-Pakistan tone. On the contrary, he spoke rather fondly of his years in Islamabad. When the Pakistani delegate to the conference arrived, later than the rest, Lambha was one of the few people to show him any kindness.

The Pakistani position in Bonn was unenviable. The conference had brought together all the major strands of the Afghan opposition, that is, those opposed to the regime Pakistan had installed and supported. Almost without exception the Afghans in the Petersberg were hostile to Pakistan, as were all the regional governments represented there, to varying degrees. Islamabad exacerbated this problem by selecting as its conference representative a comparatively junior official who, until a few weeks earlier, had been its ambassador to Kabul, that is, to the Taliban. Some of the Afghans took this choice as a calculated discourtesy. It certainly seemed insensitive. I suspected, however, that the real reason Islamabad sent him was that none of the more senior Pakistani Foreign Ministry officials were willing to accept the uncongenial assignment. Throughout the next few days I would occasionally encounter this poor fellow sitting by himself in one of the conference center's least frequented lounges, an isolated and forlorn figure.

Moscow sent a personable middle-ranking diplomat with extensive experience in Central Asia. Of Uzbek ancestry but thoroughly Russified, Zamir Kabulov was clearly under instructions to be helpful. His cooperation represented a welcome change from the Russian attitude I had encountered during the Kosovo negotiations at the Petersberg. Kabulov was, however, pessimistic about our chances of achieving this conference's objectives. Moscow read the Northern Alliance leadership, with whom it had intimate ties, as badly divided over the power-sharing formula we would be pushing. Some UN staffers believed that the Russians were backing Rabbani's effort to hold on to the Afghan presidency. Whether this assertion was true or not, Kabulov and I tended to go over the same ground every meeting. I would insist that we should not leave Bonn without an agreement on a new Afghan government, and Kabulov would reply that we would need several more conferences extending over many months to achieve that result.

My optimism reflected a professional lifetime of mostly successful multilateral diplomacy. As the world's most powerful country, the United States tended to succeed in enterprises to which it was really committed—as it now was to the Afghan intervention—particularly when it operated with broad international backing. I also had Abdullah's assurances that he, Defense Minister Fahim, and Interior Minister Qanooni were ready to support the choice of a new president drawn from outside the Northern Alliance. Thus I spent the next ten days wondering if my Russian colleague's pessimism reflected better information than my own or if he had unstated reservations about the direction in which I hoped to drive the conference. In the end Kabulov and his foreign minister would play decisive roles.

THE EVENING BEFORE the conference opened, my staff received a call from the Iranian delegation, which had just arrived from Tehran. The Iranians wanted to know if I would meet them at their hotel. I had forewarned Washington of my intention to try and work with the Iranians, and I had asked Brahimi to apprise Tehran of my position. Hence the Iranians' invitation was not a complete surprise. I was encouraged, however, that they had taken the initiative rather than waited for me to make the first move.

Khalilzad and Luti were both with me when I received the Iranians' message. Both wanted to attend the meeting. Like any forbidden fruit, talking with representatives of the Iranian Revolution held a particular fascination. I asked Khalilzad to come with me. Because he spoke Farsi or at least the Afghan version, which was not all that different, he could prove useful. I was also fairly confident that Zal would follow my lead. I was less sure about Luti, who I knew was excitable on the topic of Iran and strongly opposed to any dialogue with its government. Although not included in my invitation, Luti walked purposefully with us toward the waiting car, thus forcing me to explain that I did not think it was a good idea for a DOD representative to join the talks at this stage.

"I have Colin Powell's approval to talk to the Iranians," I said by way of explanation. "I am not sure you have Don Rumsfeld's."

Khalilzad and I drove across the river to the Iranians' hotel. We called from the lobby and were shown to their suite. Javad Zarif, the head of their delegation, had not yet arrived, but three of his colleagues were there to greet us, including Muhammad Ibrahim Taherian, the Iranian ambassador to the Northern Alliance for the past several years.

We spent an hour getting acquainted and comparing notes. Our appraisals of the situation and our stated objectives appeared to match. We both wanted to emerge from Bonn with an agreement on the identity of a new Afghan government. We assumed that the Northern Alliance would provide the core of this government, but we also recognized the need to include a significant number of figures from the other main factions. The Iranians thought the new head of the government would have to be someone outside the Northern Alliance. They were opposed to Zahir Shah playing this role, however, because of his age, his infirmity, and his indecisiveness in the best of times. Hamid Karzai was one name they had heard as a possible candidate for this position. They told me Karzai was known favorably in Tehran and would be acceptable to them.

Both Lambha and Kabulov had spoken positively about Karzai with me earlier that day. Now, with the Iranians proposing him as well, a bandwagon seemed to be rolling.

I agreed that the former king was not a good candidate to lead the new regime, given his age and his disinclination to assume the role. Because Zahir did seem to be popular throughout Afghanistan, however, I wondered whether he could play some symbolic role and add a source of national unity. The Iranian diplomats seemed to accept this idea, or at least they did not reject it. Subsequently I learned that any role, however limited, for the former king would encounter strong resistance from Tehran's revolutionary regime, whose legitimacy stemmed from its overthrow of Iran's own monarch. From the revolutionary Islamic Republic of Iran's standpoint, one restored shah in the region would be one too many.

THE FOLLOWING MORNING I briefed my delegation about this discussion. Luti's subordinate, Harold Rohde, became agitated this time. He rejected the possibility that even a tactical convergence of interest between Tehran and Washington might exist. Luti was calmer but equally censorious. I was not unhappy, therefore, when Bill told me that they both would be returning to Washington the next day.

Several years later I learned that Luti, Rohde, and Larry Franklin had all been busy arranging contacts with violent opponents of the Iranian regime even as the Bonn Conference was under way. Their first meeting took place in Rome while the rest of us were at the Petersberg. These DOD emissaries acted without State Department or White House sanction. Further, according to George Tenet's memoir, they broached the possibility of U.S. financial support for their interlocutors' efforts to overthrow the Iranian regime and of channeling this money through the Pentagon rather than through the State

Department or the CIA. On learning of these contacts, Tenet and Powell both tried, without entire success, to close down this channel.

I was even more surprised to read several years later of Larry Franklin's arrest by the FBI and his subsequent conviction for espionage. He had been charged with transmitting secret documents about Iran to pro-Israeli lobbyists who passed them in turn to the Israeli Embassy. While Luti and Rohde had been vocally opposed to any dealings with the Iranian regime, Franklin had been quiet and self-contained throughout his time with us. He had never expressed an opinion on Iran or any other substantive issue.

7

AT THE PETERSBERG

JOSCHKA FISCHER OPENED the Bonn Conference on the morning of November 27. Then Brahimi and the leaders of the four Afghan delegations gave their remarks. The tone was upbeat. The Afghans avoided recrimination and spoke in positive terms about their desire to cooperate in forging a new Afghan government. Interior Minister Younis Qanooni, the top Northern Alliance representative, was particularly conciliatory. His speech was encouraging, as his faction already controlled much of the country. At Brahimi's initiative, Hamid Karzai participated briefly by satellite telephone from the outskirts of Kandahar, where his insurgent band was seeking to oust Mullah Omar from this last city still in Taliban hands. None of the opening presentations were in Pashto, thus adding to the perception that the Pashtuns were underrepresented.

OBSERVING THE VARIOUS Afghan delegations' arrival in the previous several days, I had been pleasantly surprised by the warmth with which the members of competing factions had greeted one another. The atmosphere sometimes approached that of an extended family reunion, as indeed it was for some. I wondered if the ethnic and religious divisions within Afghan society might be less deep seated than those I had encountered in the Balkans and would later observe in Iraq. My impression was reinforced through conversations with numerous Afghan leaders, as I sought to explore the basis for their disagreements. With Serb, Croat, and Muslim communities in the Balkans, such inquiries invariably elicited a list of grievances going back a millennium.

With the Afghans, by contrast, the perceived sources of sectarian conflict were much more recent, dating from the fall of the monarchy and the Soviet Union's intervention in 1979. They recalled earlier eras, however inaccurately, as times of ethnic harmony and national unity.

I arranged meetings with the leader of each Afghan faction as the group arrived. The two most important were the Northern Alliance and the royalists, or Rome group. Younis Qanooni, whom I had first encountered in Bagram, led the former, and Dr. Abdul Sattar Sirat, a professor of Islamic theology who had participated in my meeting with Zahir Shah two weeks previously, headed the latter.

Qanooni was a small, dapperly dressed man in his late thirties. He walked with a slight limp, dressed with casual style, and projected an alert, good-humored air. Like Abdullah, Qanooni was a protégé of the assassinated Tajik warlord Ahmed Shah Massoud. His limp was the result of a failed attempt on his life by Gulbuddin Hekmatyar, an extremist mujahideen leader whose son-in-law, by coincidence, headed the Cyprus delegation to this very meeting. As the Northern Alliance's interior minister, Qanooni controlled its police forces. Thus, while not precisely a warlord, he did exercise considerable authority.

Sirat was an older man; indeed, he had served as justice minister under the monarchy some thirty years earlier. He was a respected scholar of Islamic law, which he taught at a Saudi university.

The Northern Alliance's delegation was organized more or less hierarchically; consequently, I could do most of my business with its leader. The main factions within the alliance were represented, and all needed to agree. Within limits, however, I could rely on Qanooni to do that. The other three groups were collections of individuals and needed to be dealt with as such. I had met only a few of the delegates before, but members of my team knew most them. Thus we would cultivate and expand these contacts over the next few days.

Both the Rome and Peshawar delegations were made up largely of émigrés, many of whom came from prominent families and were well educated and Westernized in dress and manner. We did encounter a few more colorful figures. One was Pacha Khan Zadran, an imposing personality with an amazingly craggy face and sweeping black mustache. He was always accoutred in full tribal regalia, including an enormous turban, and presented the very picture of a brigand chieftain circa 1850.

Both of these predominantly Pashtun delegations were highly suspicious of the Northern Alliance, which controlled all but one of the country's major cities and consequently thought itself entitled to dominate any new government. The Northern Alliance representatives, for their part, resented that they were far outnumbered by the other three groups. They required constant assurances that the number of seats allocated at the conference would not prejudice the eventual distribution of ministerial portfolios.

The smallest delegation, known as the Cyprus group, comprised somewhat younger émigré intellectuals said to have ties to Iran. If so, it was manifested only in their generally constructive attitude and the absence of evident personal ambition.

I had expected Abdullah to head the Northern Alliance team and was consequently upset when he had sent Qanooni instead. The interior minister did not speak English. This problem was not insuperable, but it was an obstacle to entirely candid exchanges, since some third party would always witness any of our conversations. More important, Abdullah and I had established a degree of mutual confidence during our time together in Tashkent, Bagram, and the flight between them. Qanooni represented the same Panjshiri faction as Abdullah, but whether he would prove equally candid and reliable I could not tell. I therefore asked Phil Mudd to get a message to Abdullah, through Gary Berntsen, asking the foreign minister to come to Bonn.

Abdullah's answer arrived a few hours later. He would come if I insisted, but he also had important things to do in Kabul. Mudd and Berntsen arranged a phone call for us. Abdullah said he would travel to Bonn if I thought it was important, but he suggested he might be more useful staying with the rest of the leadership in Kabul, from which Qanooni would be receiving his instructions. Reluctantly, I could see his argument made sense. Any agreement in Bonn would require concessions on all sides, and Qanooni would require authorization to make these compromises. The alliance's one necessary concession would be losing the presidency, which Rabbani could be expected to oppose. I therefore agreed that Abdullah should remain in Kabul and arranged that we would talk by telephone from time to time.

OVER THE NEXT several days the conference fell into something of a routine. Brahimi chaired the Afghan sessions and led their discussions over a series of hurdles. First, they spent a day or two clearing their throats, giving all the delegates an opportunity to express their hopes for the meeting. Once everyone had had his say, Brahimi surfaced the first draft of what he hoped would be an agreed final document, one intended to serve as an interim constitution for the new government. Then followed nearly a week of negotiations on that government's form and functions. Finally, as the conference went into overtime, Brahimi moved to secure their agreement on the actual personalities to fill its top posts.

National delegations had access to the site but not to the formal meetings. Because we were all eating and taking our leisure in the same facility, we had ample opportunities for interaction with the Afghan delegates over meals, coffee, or walks in the garden during rare breaks in the cold, gloomy, wet weather. In this manner the essentially Afghan nature of the negotiations was preserved, and at the same time the interested governments had an opportunity to influence the results. Whether this arrangement proved beneficial would depend, obviously, on the nature of that influence and the degree to which it was exerted in a convergent fashion. Brahimi took the lead in moving the Afghans toward our desired goals while I did the same with the international representatives. Brahimi and I could call on each other to overcome some particular obstacle, however, and often did so.

The meeting took place in the midst of Ramadan, the holy month during which devout Muslims fast throughout the day. Most Muslims attending the conference observed the fast, so the dining room was empty of delegates from dawn to dusk. However secular some of the more cosmopolitan figures might have been in private life, all were on their most devout behavior throughout their stay at the Petersberg. An exception, interesting enough, was the Iranian delegation. Its members availed themselves of their Shia religion's more liberal provision for travelers, which allowed them to postpone their fast until they returned home.

Most of the Afghans rose late in the day and worked late into the night. The international delegates, myself included, tended to keep more normal hours. Before most of the Afghans awoke, we spent our mornings talking over the previous day's events and discussing how best to influence those of the next day. Through the afternoon and evening we would meet with various Afghan delegates and discuss the upcoming items on the conference agenda. After dinner, the Afghans would go into late-night sessions, to which we did not have entrée, and we could go to bed. I arranged, however, for one or two U.S. delegation members to remain on duty each evening till the last Afghan had retired so that I could begin the next day fully informed of the previous night's developments.

From the Congress of Vienna in 1815 to the Dayton Peace Conference of 1995, many breakthroughs have been achieved over a good meal and generous measure of spirits. This Bonn meeting had to proceed without the benefit of either. The Muslim delegates did not consume alcohol, and in observing Ramadan, there was little food, at least in daylight. Finally, most of the participants had come from halfway around the world and were consequently jet lagged more than usual. How successful, I wondered, could an international conference be at which everyone was sober, hungry, and tired.

Only Khalilzad, Karp, and I were accommodated at the Petersberg. Thus in the afternoons, I drove down the hill to meet with the rest of my delegation, go through the message traffic with Washington, and provide guidance for the next day's events. Like a basketball coach, I had my team playing a combination of a zone and man-to-man defense. Garry Robbins, the political officer from Rome, was assigned to keep track of the royalist delegation, and Roger Kenna, who had organized our program in Peshawar, looked after those Afghans who had traveled from Pakistan. I assigned others to the Northern Alliance and Cyprus delegations. At the same time, I organized my small force into shifts, so that some Americans would always be trolling the lounges from early morning till late in the evening.

Before returning to the Petersberg each evening, I briefed the American and other international journalists covering the conference. Reporters could not access the site, and the UN spokesman's daily press conference was intentionally uninformative. Brahimi did not want the individual Afghans playing for the gallery and felt that compromises would be easier to strike if the process was not subjected to excessive scrutiny. I agreed, but I also wanted to use the media to keep the pressure on the Afghans to make those compromises.

The press simply wanted a story, of course, as accurate and complete as possible. I therefore provided a bit more information than the UN spokesman but usually just on background. I allowed the journalists to quote an unidentified "international observer" but not to cite me by name or to attribute the information to an American source. In this manner, I sought to keep the United Nations at the center of the process, to put pressure on the Afghans to make progress, and to minimize the apparent American role.

Night would fall by the time I drove back up the hill. The Afghans would be up and about, meeting in plenary, caucusing with their various delegations, or holding quiet talks in small groups spread around the conference site's several lounges. Issues unresolved in the previous evening's plenary would be up for further negotiation. Brahimi and I would meet to review the latest obstacles to progress and consider how they might be overcome. Our discussion would normally lead to some division of labor. Brahimi would work on some individuals and I on others. We would also bring other international representatives into the process and have them press those with whom they had the greatest influence. Usually these combinations would work. By the following morning, more points at issue would have been resolved, and we would have advanced further toward our goal.

Dinner was the main social gathering, being the only meal most of the Afghans could join. We ate in a single large dining room gathered around multiple round tables, each seating perhaps a dozen. Service was buffet style, and the cuisine's variety, quantity, and quality were excellent. Over the many dishes was a large sign assuring us, in several languages, that none of the food contained pork. People sat down in their order of arrival, so one tended to have different companions for each meal. This being Europe, wine was available, but most stuck to mineral water, juice, or soft drinks.

Following dinner, events slowed down. Because Washington was still at work, I checked in with home base while Brahimi and the Afghans spent another three or four hours in plenary session. One or two of my colleagues remained alert for reports on the latest developments. I could go to sleep before too long, confident of a full briefing on the evening's events first thing in the morning.

The large dining room was often nearly empty for breakfast. On several occasions, seeing that Zarif and his Iranian colleagues had a large table to themselves, I made it a point to join them. They seemed a little startled the first time but by no means discomfited.

We also met with the Iranians in a slightly larger format each morning at ten o'clock. In addition to Khalilzad and myself, this mid-morning coffee included the Italian and German representatives. This format was a vestige of the Italian and German governments' earlier efforts, with UN encouragement, to foster a U.S.-Iranian dialogue on Afghanistan. Strictly speaking, these coffees were no longer necessary, as our two sides now communicated directly, but I saw no reason to disappoint the European matchmakers. These daily sessions in fact proved quite useful.

ONE MORNING, several days into the conference, we all sat around with our coffee and cakes and reviewed the first draft of what was intended to be the gathering's final agreement, which Brahimi had circulated the previous evening. Javad Zarif, who had gone over the document already, said that it seemed to be missing a couple of elements.

"Oh?" I responded noncommittally. I did not want to admit that I had not yet read through it myself.

"The text makes no mention of democratic elections," Zarif said, with a twinkle in his eye. "Don't you think that the new Afghan regime should be committed to hold democratic elections?"

It was hard to disagree with this proposition. On the one hand, the Bush administration had not yet embraced democratization as its strategy for dampening support for extremism throughout the Middle East. My instructions only called for forming a broadly based, representative regime in Kabul. On the other hand, there did not seem any harm in Zarif's suggestion. "Yes, of course," I agreed.

"Furthermore," Zarif continued, "the draft makes no mention of terrorism. Should we not insist that the new Afghan regime be committed to cooperate with the international community to combat terrorism?"

Zarif was having some fun at my expense, co-opting themes more usually connected with American than Iranian policy; however, he was also making a point. While Washington was fond of characterizing the Iranian regime as a fundamentalist theocracy, the truth was more complex. Iran wasn't Switzerland, but its government was more democratic than Egypt's and less fundamentalist than Saudi Arabia's, two of America's most important allies in the region. Iran's Parliament and president were popularly elected in hard-fought contests, the most recent of which had installed the then-moderate, reformist regime that Zarif represented. A council of popularly elected clerics even chose the country's supreme leader, the successor to Ayatollah Khomeini. None of these ballots was entirely free or fair, but the Iranian people had more influence over the choice of their leaders than most other societies in the Middle East.

Regarding terrorism, Tehran had long been an opponent of both the Taliban and al Qaeda. Insofar as Afghanistan was concerned, therefore, Zarif was perfectly sincere in his pro-democracy, antiterrorism stance. For Afghanistan, his government did want to see free elections held and al Qaeda's influence eliminated. Had we been addressing the situations in Lebanon or the Palestinian territories, U.S. and Iranian views on democracy and terrorism would be further apart. For Afghanistan, however, our objectives were similar. In due course the Afghans incorporated Zarif's suggestions into the Bonn Agreement.

DAY BY DAY the contents of this document took final shape. The parties agreed that for the next six months an Interim Administration, whose members would be selected at the Petersberg, should govern Afghanistan. At the end of the six-month period, a loya jirga would meet and name the Interim Administration's replacement, forming a transitional government that would carry on for another eighteen months. The transitional government would draft a new constitution and organize national elections. Thus while the government chosen in Bonn would last only six months, its leadership would have a hand in picking the successor regime and in organizing the national elections.

As usual in such negotiations, everyone put off till last the most controversial issues. Among these matters were determining the proposed role of the former king, selecting the Interim Administration's chairman, and distributing the ministerial-level portfolios within that body. The Rome group wanted to name Zahir Shah the head of state and insisted that among his prerogatives should be choosing the head of the Interim Administration. Several European governments, including Italy's, supported this view. Not surprising, the Iranians and the Northern Alliance were adamantly opposed.

Washington had no strong views on this point, so I exercised my discretion. For almost all the issues discussed in Bonn, I had no written instructions and a good deal of leeway. My job was to get an agreement and almost any agreement would do, so long as it resulted in an Afghan government that would replace the Taliban's, unite the opposition, secure international support, cooperate in hunting down al Qaeda's remnants, and relieve the United States of the need to occupy and run the country.

Up to this point in the conference, eager as I was to enhance the Afghan content of the eventual arrangement and maintain its broader international auspices, I had avoided any substantive involvement. Nearly a week's effort had produced no progress on these central issues, however, and clearly any further deadlock could cause the whole effort to unravel. One delegate, Haji Qadir, had already abandoned the conference in a well-publicized huff, claiming that Pashtuns were underrepresented. Qadir himself was not a great loss, but further defections could undermine the whole process's credibility.

Having slept on the matter, I awoke with a scheme that I thought might solve all three of the most troublesome pending issues at once. Checking first with Brahimi, I described my proposal. The former king should be asked to open the loya jirga that would meet six months after the Bonn meeting's conclusion. Next, the Rome group should be accorded the privilege of nominating the head of the Interim Administration, provided that it put forward a candidate acceptable to the other three factions. Finally, we should drop the effort to form an interim council as well.

I based my proposal on four calculations. First, Zahir would be content with his rather modest formal role in this scheme. Second, the Northern Alliance, and the Iranians, would likewise accept Zahir's role. Next, the Rome group's potential candidate for the head of the Interim Administration, Hamid Karzai, would prove acceptable to the other three groups. Last, it would be easier to get the assembled Afghans to agree on the membership of one body, rather than two, within our limited remaining time.

With Brahimi's blessing, Khalilzad and I set about validating these assumptions. Khalilzad knew Zahir better than I; therefore, he telephoned the former king in Rome. Zahir proved amenable to the part foreseen for him under this scheme. Once again, he emphasized that he did not have any personal ambition. He only wanted to promote national reconciliation and live out his remaining years in his native land.

Khalilzad and I then went to see Qanooni, who likewise quickly fell in with the scheme. Like Abdullah, he recognized that the Northern Alliance alone could not hope to lead a broadly based government that would enjoy widespread support at home and legitimacy abroad. In this aspect, both Qanooni and Abdullah reflected the view of their slain leader, Ahmed Shah Massoud, but not necessarily that of the other Northern Alliance factions.

I anticipated the greatest difficulty would be in selling my proposal to the Rome group, which would have to abandon its vision of a restored monarchy. I met with Dr. Sirat, the head of the Rome delegation, in my suite's sitting room. I presented the package in as positive a light as possible, noting that the former king would be the only individual so singled out in the Bonn declaration, that the loya jirga that he would open would be free to perpetuate or expand his future role, and that acting through the Rome delegation, the former king would effectively nominate the head of the Interim Administration. I made it clear that Brahimi backed the proposal and that we had also discussed it with Zahir Shah and received his support.

In the course of the afternoon Khalilzad and I met with each of the Afghan delegations and most of the international observers to explain the proposal. Khalilzad was particularly effective in larger meetings, as a number of the Afghans did not speak English. Because he could communicate without an interpreter, he greatly expanded our diplomacy's reach. His skills would become even more important over the next few days, as we reached out to several key figures still in Afghanistan.

By day's end we had brought all the factions on board. That evening Brahimi surfaced the new arrangement in the plenary session, where it was adopted. The Bonn Agreement was amended to read that the assembled Afghan representatives had requested His Majesty Mohammed Zahir, the former king of Afghanistan, to head the Interim Administration, but that he had declined and had asked instead that they choose another candidate. Fur-

The author surrounded by his security team on the tarmac at Bagram,
November 19, 2001. The ruined control tower is in the background.
Foreign Service officer Craig Karp stands to the far right. *C. Karp*

Ambassador Dobbins emerging from the Kabul bunker on December 17
to officiate at the formal reopening of the U.S. Embassy. *C. Karp*

First call on Hamid Karzai at the Presidential Palace, December 16. *C. Karp*

Dobbins and Gen. Tommy Franks assemble in front of the embassy on their way to Karzai's inauguration, December 22. *C. Karp*

The ambassador's residence at the Kabul embassy. In addition to the bed, the embassy's only desk, computer, and telephone are on display. *C. Karp*

The new Afghan government is sworn in on December 22, before
a portrait of fallen warlord Ahmed Shah Masoud. Interior Minister
Younis Qanooni stands on the far right. Defense Minister
Mohammed Fahim is the fourth from the right. *C. Karp*

ther, His Majesty would officiate at the opening of the first loya jirga under the new regime.

HAMID KARZAI telephoned me several times during the conference. The calls were arranged through the CIA paramilitary team that was supporting his insurgent band on the outskirts of Kandahar. On one occasion, Karzai had suffered a near miss from an errant American bomb, one that killed several of his party, moments before our call. I did not detect any stress in his demeanor, which was calm, matter of fact, and unassuming. He had a deep, warm voice and spoke a slightly accented, rather elegant English, the product of an Indian university education. He reported on his efforts to liberate Kandahar and its environs and did not mention his own future. For my part, I briefed him on the discussions' progress at the Petersberg. In our last telephone call, I told him that a consensus was forming regarding his candidacy for the interim leadership. This development probably came as no great surprise to him, since his brother was a member of the Rome group participating in the Bonn meeting.

SECURITY WAS a major preoccupation for most of the Afghan delegates, particularly for those who hoped to return to Kabul in an official capacity. They had little confidence in the Northern Alliance's capability to provide for their safety and feared the alliance would intimidate them. As it developed, two of the ministers appointed in Bonn were murdered during the following year, so these fears were by no means fanciful. Further, the Northern Alliance itself was not an entirely unified movement. Renewed conflict among its competing commanders was a real possibility.

Many participants felt that an international peacekeeping force would be needed in Afghanistan both to safeguard the new government's integrity and to forestall a civil war. The Bush administration, however, was unenthusiastic about peacekeeping in general and about sending foreign troops to Afghanistan in particular. Yet without strong U.S. backing, finding other volunteers for such a mission would be difficult. The country was remote, the terrain rough, and the population large, heavily armed, and thought to be highly xenophobic.

The British representative in Bonn was Robert Cooper, an independently minded diplomat assigned to Prime Minister Tony Blair's staff in the Cabinet Office. Convinced that a peacekeeping component to the agreement we were seeking was necessary, Cooper worked with me to produce it. Neither of us had instructions on the subject, but he thought that Prime Minister Blair would agree to dispatch a British contingent to form the core of this force if both the Afghans and Washington requested it. British leadership of the force was likely to reassure the American administration, which did not want to take on the task itself but was leery about being drawn into supporting an ineffectual or amateurish operation. Among the various possibilities, a U.K.- led force was likely to be the most proficient and self-sufficient. Other than the United States, Great Britain was also the only country likely to be able to deploy the needed force quickly enough. A small British force was already operating in Afghanistan, and the United Kingdom, alone among American allies, had begun to establish the logistics network necessary to sustain its troops.

Operating somewhat in advance of our respective capitals, Cooper and I worked this issue to a satisfactory resolution, at least insofar as the current negotiations' immediate needs were concerned. In the final document, the Afghans requested that the international community dispatch a multinational force, the size and composition of which was left unspecified, to secure Kabul and later perhaps the rest of the country. Most of the delegates wanted peacekeepers deployed countrywide. This faction included some Northern Alliance representatives, who didn't see why they had to accept foreign troops in Kabul, on their turf, while other areas of the country not under Northern Alliance control remained unconstrained. Neither London nor Washington would countenance such a wider request, however. Cooper and I thus persuaded the Afghans to approach their objective one step at a time, with a force first in Kabul and later perhaps beyond.

No sooner did I feel this issue had been resolved than I read in my morning newspaper quotes from Iranian foreign minister Kharrazi questioning the need for international peacekeepers. At breakfast, I encountered Zarif. "Why," I inquired, "is your minister opposing an international security force for Kabul after you and I agreed that one is necessary?"

Zarif laughed. "Just regard my minister's remarks as a gesture of solidarity with Don Rumsfeld," he joked. "After all, Jim, we are both way out ahead of our instructions on this issue, aren't we?"

I admitted he was right. I was satisfied that Zarif would not try to undo the arrangement that had been reached.

EVERYTHING WAS now settled save the distribution of the new government's posts and, in particular, the identity of its chief. Among the international representatives was a strong consensus in favor of Hamid Karzai for the leader. This accord was by no means my doing. On the contrary, virtually every foreign official with whom I had met in the past month, including the Pakistani, the Indian, the Russian, the Iranian, the Turkish, and European delegates, had mentioned his name to me unprompted.

The unanimity of international support for Karzai was largely Dr. Abdullah's doing. He and Karzai had served together in an earlier coalition government in Kabul. He thus knew Karzai as a moderate, personable, conciliatory figure of the sort who might be able to hold a fractious coalition together. In addition to promoting Karzai's candidacy to me, Abdullah had planted the suggestion with the Russians, Indians, Iranians, Turks, and various European government officials. The Pakistanis presumably came to the idea on their own, as Abdullah was the last person from whom they would accept advice. Of course, these seeds would not have taken root if Karzai himself had not demonstrated to a wide range of disparate governments that he had the right mix of personal qualities needed to unite his war-torn country. For several years he had traveled extensively as the Afghan opposition's roving ambassador, and he had obviously made a positive impression wherever he went.

Oddly enough, the one faction in Bonn that proved least ready to jump onto the Karzai bandwagon was his own—the royalists, or Rome group. This delegation contained several older and more experienced personalities who regarded Karzai as a relative newcomer; instead, they fancied themselves for the top position. Their position did not seem to reflect any hostility to Karzai per se but indicated rather the personal ambitions of men who, in their view, had a greater claim on the highest office. After a couple of days in internal discussion, the group nominated its leader, Professor Abdul Sattar Sirat, for the chairmanship of the Interim Administration.

A scholar of Islamic law, Sirat appeared bookish and exhibited an erudite manner. He came from a distinguished family and was highly respected for his learning. In his late sixties, he had served as the justice minister in the last royal government some thirty years earlier. Nothing in his appearance or background conveyed charisma, popular appeal, or leadership skills, all of which the next Afghan leader would need. Further, he was of mixed Uzbek-Pashtun background, whereas Hamid Karzai was a Popalzai Pashtun, scion of one of the country's most prominent families and important tribes. Sirat's selection thus would not reassure a Pashtun community that already claimed to be underrepresented.

In according the Rome group the privilege of nominating the head of the Interim Administration, we had stipulated that its choice had to be acceptable to all the other groups. To secure Karzai's nomination therefore, one or more of these groups would have to veto the Sirat candidacy. Few outside the Rome group were enthusiastic about Sirat, and even within that delegation several thought themselves better qualified for the position. No one, however, seemed prepared to step forward and openly oppose Sirat's nomination. This rather odd deference reflected the complex personal relationships that underlay the political competition among the various factions. Qanooni, for instance, said he much preferred Karzai, but he could not veto Sirat because the latter was a most respectable individual and, moreover, his cousin by marriage.

At this point, I began to wonder whether I had been too clever by half in proposing to accord the Rome group the privilege of nominating Afghanistan's next leader. If the conference acquiesced in Sirat, most participants would do so without enthusiasm. Neither the international community nor the population of Afghanistan seemed likely to rally around this figure from an earlier age. Northern Alliance warlords such as Fahim, Ismail Khan, and Dostum might not support the outcome, and then Rabbani might not feel compelled to step aside. A half-hearted agreement on Sirat might produce the worst possible outcome, or two rival presidents.

In the end, Brahimi broke this particular logjam. In a private meeting with Sirat, Brahimi informed him that his nomination could not succeed. Quite upset, Sirat then turned for solace to Thomas Matussek, who gave him the same advice. Finally persuaded, Sirat withdrew his candidacy.

At this point, several other less-than-optimal candidates among the Rome delegation emerged, eager to throw their hats in the ring. Khalilzad again telephoned Zahir Shah and asked for his help in restraining his supporters. Gradually one aspirant after another was dissuaded from pursuing his candidacy. Finally, the Rome group settled on its only adherent that all the other factions were ready to fully support.

ALTHOUGH MY exchanges with Zarif and his Iranian colleagues had been generally constructive, I remained concerned about their follow-through. Several Afghan delegates with strong ties to Tehran, in particular those from the Hazara community of Afghan Shias, continued to resist on points that Zarif and I had argued. In discussions with these Afghans I pointed out that the American and Iranian delegations were of one mind on these issues. My interlocutors responded with disbelief.

"You are naive to believe that the Iranians are supporting the same position as you," one of the Shia leaders told me.

During my next morning coffee with the German, Italian, and Iranian representatives, I recounted this conversation. I cautioned, "If we are to succeed here, we will need to be straight with each other. When we disagree, we should acknowledge and discuss our differences. When we are in accord, we should do our best to give effect to that agreement. If we all do not do our utmost to promote a conclusive outcome here in Bonn, this effort will falter, and it will be a long time before we get a second chance."

Zarif and his colleagues listened carefully and made no objection. My sense was that they probably had been relying on the American side to carry the burden of pressing unpalatable propositions on the Afghans. The Iranians were likely also a good deal more concerned about even a minimal role for the former king than they had let on in their conversations with me. They may have felt that openly acknowledging this anxiety would have betrayed a weakness that the U.S. side could have exploited. Nothing was further from my own intentions; however, several of the European delegations did openly favor a royal restoration, making the Iranian delegation wary.

Whatever transpired before, Zarif and his colleagues seemed to take my appeal seriously. When we checked the next day with the Afghans in question, they confirmed that the Iranian and American positions were now aligned.

BY THIS TIME we had reached the tenth day of what was supposed to have been a weeklong conference. We had concluded a tentative agreement on an interim constitution and on the individual who would head the government it created. We still had not made any progress, however, on identifying the two dozen or so individuals who would make up Karzai's cabinet and head the various government departments. Brahimi had asked each of the four groups to give him a list of their candidates for these offices. From these four lists he would seek to compose a balanced slate on which he would then try to get a consensus. All four groups had agreed to this process, but none would put forward its list until the others were ready to do so as well.

For three of the groups this exercise required only that they submit the names of their adherents who aspired to political office. For the Northern Alliance, the task was considerably more complicated. To begin with, their people already headed all the various ministries, and many would have to give up their positions. Second, the alliance comprised half a dozen or more substantial military contingents, each headed by a commander who would insist that he or his supporters should share in the spoils of office.

Then we faced the problem of President Rabbani. This gentleman understood that whoever else might gain by this nominating process, he could only lose. He was not disposed to lose; consequently, he refused to allow Qanooni to put forward any names.

Over the next several days the conference spun its wheels while Qanooni sought instructions that would allow him to proceed. None were forthcoming. With most other elements of the package provisionally agreed, the delegates did not have much to do. Participants had already extended their stays in Bonn several days longer than anticipated. Many became restless. The longer this unwelcome pause continued, the more likely existing bargains would be reopened, key figures would drift off, and the meeting would end inconclusively.

Qanooni finally asked to see me. He said that discussions within his Kabul leadership were deadlocked. He saw no prospect that this impasse could be quickly overcome. He proposed to adjourn the Bonn Conference for a week or two, during which he would return to Afghanistan and try to secure an agreement to proceed with the new government's selection.

Qanooni's proposal made some sense. We had an agreed framework upon which a new government could be formed, what amounted to an interim constitution. If the Bonn meeting adjourned, we would have accomplished something. I was deeply worried, however, that if this gathering broke up, reassembling the same group and picking up where it had left off would be nearly impossible. Once again we would have to parley over where and when to meet and whom to invite. Each faction would return with new demands and new reservations about bargains already struck. In the meantime, events in Afghanistan might move toward new conflicts between Pashtun and Northern Alliance elements or even within the alliance itself.

Leaving Qanooni, I walked into the park surrounding the conference center where the cell phone reception was better. The sky was overcast, as it had been for most of the week, and a light mist enveloped me. I called the State Department and spoke with Richard Armitage. I told him about Qanooni's proposal and explained the pros and cons. A few minutes later he called back, having spoken with Powell. The secretary was not ready to throw in the towel, Armitage reported. Instead, I should hold everyone in Bonn while Powell worked the telephones to muster a broader international effort to break the logjam in Kabul.

I went back inside and conveyed the results of my conversation to Qanooni, who reacted with relief. Clearly he had not been fully persuaded by his own proposal, recognizing as I did the dangers inherent in any premature break up of the Bonn gathering.

I then spoke individually to the other key envoys—the Russians, Indians, and Iranians—and clearly stated that the moment of decision had come and that Washington would help persuade the Northern Alliance leadership to table its list of candidates. I also met with German foreign minister Joschka Fischer, who was visiting the conference site, and asked for his assistance. Meanwhile, Khalilzad spoke by satellite telephone with two of the principal warlords, Abdul Rashid Dostum and Ismail Khan, both of whom expressed their support for the effort under way in Bonn. Gen. Fahim Khan and I also exchanged written messages to the same effect. I called Foreign Minister Abdullah in Kabul to update him on our efforts. Finally, Khalilzad spoke directly with President Rabbani by telephone, reiterating the dire consequences for Afghanistan if the Bonn meeting did not succeed. Fischer called Rabbani as well. Both stressed our need to proceed and form a new government under new leadership. In Washington, Powell made calls to enlist others with possible influence over the Northern Alliance. Among those he called was Russian foreign minister Igor Ivanov.

Later that afternoon, I gave a press conference. For the first time I spoke on the record, not afraid to show a bit of obvious American pressure. If the Bonn Conference failed, I wanted there to be no doubt where the responsibility lay. I made it clear that President Rabbani was the obstacle.

By the following morning the dam had broken. The critical moment came, Abdullah later told me, when the Russian ambassador interrupted a Northern Alliance leadership meeting with urgent instructions from Moscow. The Russian government wanted the Northern Alliance to understand, his message said, that if it did not accept the package that was now on the table in Bonn, it would receive no further Russian aid. This key long-term supporter's blunt ultimatum finally persuaded Rabbani to drop his objections and let the selection of cabinet ministers go forward.

By the following morning Qanooni had received the go-ahead to pass his list of proposed ministers to Brahimi. The other three groups did the same. Finally, the finish line was in sight. We accordingly scheduled a formal closing ceremony for the following day over which the German chancellor, Gerhard Schröder, would preside.

For the first time in weeks, I had nothing immediate to do. Brahimi had the lists and would try to compose a generally acceptable cabinet, balanced among political factions, ethnicities, and gender. The less the United States had to do with this process, the better for the resultant government's legitimacy. Seizing the opportunity for a bit of recreation, I took my first real break since arriving in Bonn. Driving into the surrounding countryside, I located a favorite hiking trail from my earlier tenure in Bonn. It wended several miles through field and forest to a steep crag at the top of which stood the ruined castle of a medieval robber baron. On a Sunday in good weather this path would have been filled with families out for their weekly constitutional, pausing for wurst or schnitzel under the trees of an outdoor beer garden. Today the ground was covered by wet snow, the sky heavily overcast, the beer garden closed, and the way entirely deserted. Walking up the long incline, I enjoyed an expansive view over the wintry landscape from the peak. On the way back I took a wrong turn and stumbled around for half an hour, lost and disoriented. Eventually I regained the path and my car, tired but greatly refreshed.

Back at the Petersberg, I found the conference center ominously quiet. Brahimi was meeting with leading members of each of the Afghan delegations and trying to work out a commonly acceptable list of cabinet ministers. As the evening wore on, suspense mounted. Well past midnight Brahimi asked to see me. Negotiations were again at an impasse. Qanooni, on instructions from Kabul, was insisting that the Northern Alliance not only occupy the three most important ministries—defense, foreign affairs, and interior—but also hold three-fourths of the total. The other groups found these terms unacceptable. Unless the Northern Alliance's demand was significantly reduced, the resultant government could not be portrayed as broadly based and representative.

Brahimi said Qanooni was adamant and could not be moved. I suggested that we collect several of the other national envoys and try to persuade Qanooni to moderate his demands. Brahimi agreed, and I rounded up those representatives who could still be found at that time of night.

Fifteen minutes later we assembled around Brahimi's dining room table. In addition to Brahimi, the group consisted of Kabulov, Lambha, Zarif, Matussek, Khalilzad, and me. Qanooni arrived, looked around the room, and saw that he was in for a difficult session. For the next two hours we took turns explaining to him why the Northern Alliance could not expect to retain the three power ministries while also insisting on holding most of the others. Qanooni responded that his faction had already conceded the most important slot, the chairmanship of the interim regime. He reminded us that he and his colleagues had been fighting for their country for the past decade while all the other claimants to office had been living in comfortable exile. He explained that the Northern Alliance was a coalition of many factions, all of which insisted on representation in the new government. This last point, we understood, was the core of his problem.

We explored several expedients. We suggested dividing existing portfolios to create more posts and proposed inventing one or two new ministries. Qanooni remained adamant. Meanwhile, the clock was ticking, the German chancellor's arrival was only hours away, and we still did not have an agreement.

Finally Zarif stood up and signaled Qanooni to join him in the corner of the room. They whispered for no more than a minute. Qanooni then returned to the table and agreed to give up two ministries. He also agreed to the creation of three new ones that would also go to other factions.

We had a deal. For the next six months an Interim Administration comprised of twenty-nine department heads plus a chairman would govern Afghanistan. Sixteen of these posts, or just slightly more than half, would go to the Northern Alliance. Twenty-nine ministries were more cabinet-level positions than Afghanistan (or any state) required, and some of the portfolios were of little importance. But we had a deal that would stick and a balanced slate that could be sold to the other factions.

I WENT BACK to my room, called Washington to confirm that the final bargain had been struck, and went to bed. Exhilaration soon gave way to exhaustion.

A few hours later, well before Chancellor Schröder's arrival, I left the Petersberg for the Frankfurt Airport and a flight to Washington. I was confident that Khalilzad and the other members of my team could deal with any last-minute issues that arose. I was also content to leave the limelight to Brahimi and the Afghans. Throughout the conference, I had done my best to play down the American role. Skipping the finale seemed an appropriate finishing touch.

Before departing I filed a concluding report to Washington in which I emphasized the critical role others played in this achievement. "The late-night session that preceded the successful conclusion of the Bonn Conference underscored why the conference ultimately worked," my final telegram read. "Neighboring states, Western governments, and the UN worked in tandem to be helpful at this meeting. Their combined weight, operating for the first time in a cohesive effort, succeeded in pushing the Afghans together."

International backing had been important to this success, and so had the support I had received from U.S. government agencies and their representatives in Bonn. Khalilzad, for one, had proven loyal, disciplined, and extremely effective. His ability to speak directly to Rabbani and several key Afghan military commanders was a major asset. Phil Mudd and his colleagues in Afghanistan had facilitated these contacts, as well as those I had enjoyed with Karzai, Fahim, and Abdullah. And, of course, American military prowess on the battlefield gave weight to our diplomacy.

On the United Airlines flight home the pilot recognized my name and came back to say how pleased he was to have me aboard. Apparently my efforts to stay out of the news had not been entirely successful. I can't say I was entirely displeased.

8

THE INAUGURATION

A WEEK LATER KARP, Mudd, Gill, and I were back at Bagram airfield. As our aircraft came to a halt, the bottom rear section of its fuselage slowly dropped to the ground. Outside the scene was pitch black, lit only by a few waving flashlights. In the distance were several other C-17s with their ramps down, looking like open maws of silent beasts in the darkness. We walked down the incline into the night, where waiting hands guided us into a large tent just off the runway. A canvas partition divided the interior. On one side we saw a dozen or so reclining bodies, some snoring lightly, and on the other was a lighted area with four picnic tables and a large urn of coffee. This was the Bagram passenger terminal and barracks.

At dawn we climbed into a couple of armored Chevrolet Suburbans for the drive to Kabul, some twenty miles distant. In addition to the team that had accompanied me on my last visit were Peter Rodman from the Office of the Secretary of Defense and Air Force Maj. Gen. Kevin Chilton from the Joint Staff. The bare and rugged landscape we traversed was reminiscent of the American Southwest, with miles of flat, parched earth in every direction and rugged mountains in the distance. We did not see any remnant of the fields, vineyards, and orchards that had filled this once-well-irrigated plain. Instead, along the road were bomb craters, blown bridges, rusted antiaircraft guns, partially demolished tanks, and deserted housing compounds. At one point we took an off-road detour around a section staked with warnings of land mines. At another point we left the road to ford a stream, passing a downed bridge.

By early morning we had arrived in town. Its streets were almost deserted. The sky was overcast and the temperature near freezing. We could make out low-lying, earth-colored buildings visible through a light haze, the byproduct of charcoal fires that provided the only source of heat for most of the population. At first glance, Kabul did not look as bad as I had anticipated. The streets were not teeming with beggars, as they had been in Port-au-Prince; the populace was not all carrying AK-47s, as they had in Mogadishu; and the buildings were not all pitted with shell holes, as they were in Sarajevo. I later learned that other areas of the city were much more heavily damaged.

Uniformed police were out and about. A few directed traffic, a somewhat superfluous activity given the absence of private automobiles; however, taxis seemed plentiful. As the day progressed more pedestrians emerged. Shops opened and sold the basics of life. Most women still wore the all-encompassing burka, which until a couple of weeks earlier had been mandatory attire for any female venturing outdoors. Men wore a mix of traditional and Western attire. A few soldiers strolled about, but they were unarmed and nonthreatening.

We drove along wide empty boulevards toward the U.S. Embassy. That building had been vacant for more than a decade. Afghan employees had continued to tend the grounds after the last American left in 1989. Almost no one had entered the building itself, save on one occasion when anti-American demonstrators had stormed the grounds and gained brief access to the embassy's interior. The main structure stood in the middle of a large walled compound. At first glance, it seemed intact and the surrounding grounds well tended. Closer inspection revealed the consequences of its neglect. The building had no heat, electricity, or water. A thick layer of dust covered every surface. Underneath the grime the interior remained as a sort of time capsule. Offices stood just as they had when their occupants departed twelve years earlier. Pictures of Ronald Reagan and George Shultz adorned the walls. Warm beer and Coca-Cola sat in the refrigerator, and a half-empty bottle of Jack Daniels stood on the bar in the basement. Dated telegrams filled in boxes, and one ashtray contained a half-smoked cigar. In the garage stood a fleet of late-1980s American sedans, at least one of which was still operable.

A company of U.S. Marines had preceded us into Kabul by several days to provide our perimeter security and had set up camp in the unheated, unlit chancellery. Also on hand to greet us was a small advance guard of State Department personnel, including a political officer, several administrative specialists, a public affairs officer, and a representative of the U.S. Agency for International Development (USAID). The majority of these hardy pioneers were women. This staffing represented a big change from my early days in the Foreign Service, which had refused to send female officers to Middle Eastern countries lest their presence should offend local sensibilities.

The State Department contingent had found shelter in an underground storage bunker a short distance from the main building. Here the plumbing and electricity still worked, and paraffin stoves somewhat precariously supplied heat. Its three small rooms served as a men's dorm, a women's dorm, and my room, which afforded me some measure of privacy. As this third room contained the building's only desk, telephone, and computer, however, I was not often alone. The bunker possessed a single toilet, sink, and shower, resulting in long morning queues.

Karp, Gill, and our security agents bunked with the marines in the chancellery building, where cots and lanterns had been rigged. Rodman and Chilton stayed with the small American military contingent located elsewhere in the city. Mudd fared best, somehow finding accommodations that included an aboveground bedroom, heat, light, plumbing, and a dining hall that served hot meals. After the first night, I considered moving in with him, but my security team scotched the idea.

This existence rather differed from the cookie-pushing, stripped-pants lifestyle usually associated with a diplomatic career. And indeed, for the first couple of decades, my own life had largely conformed to that former pattern. I had traveled to and from my first European post aboard the most opulent ocean liners. At the conclusion of such voyages, which had featured shuffleboard in the afternoon and black-tie dinners every evening, cars would offload onto the pier, and we passengers could drive the last few miles to Paris or London. I'd even worn stripped pants once, for a reception at Buckingham Palace.

With the end of the Cold War, life in the Foreign Service changed, at least for me. Instead of Paris and London, I traveled to Mogadishu, Port-au-Prince, and Sarajevo. And while I only visited these troubled spots, many of my colleagues took up residence there and in other war-torn capitals.

Getting even the simplest things done in such an environment could be a challenge. In Kabul we did not have functioning telephones. The terrestrial system had been destroyed, and cellular service had not yet been introduced. We could only make appointments by word of mouth. This process involved dispatching a runner, who would try to locate the desired interlocutor and fix a time and place for the rendezvous. We could arrange two or, at best, three appointments a day this way. Nor did we have much to do in the interval. The embassy did not have a telegraphic link to Washington, so we neither sent nor received classified messages. There were no newspapers, no radio, and no TV. So each day had its share of tedium and discomfort as well as excitement.

My main purpose in Kabul was to ensure that the transfer of power from Rabbani to Karzai went smoothly. Fortunately, the three most powerful figures in the outgoing government—Abdullah, Qanooni, and Fahim—were committed to the change. In later years I sometimes encountered criticism that this Panjshiri faction of the Northern Alliance had been awarded too great a share of power in the first post-Taliban government. At the time, it was clear to all but the most partial observer that the transfer from the Rabbani-led Northern Alliance government to the more broadly based Karzai administration would not have happened had these three individuals not promoted the change, organized the transition, and then remained in place long enough to see the new government take hold.

The other element needed to ensure a peaceful and orderly transition was the deployment of a multinational security force. On our way to Kabul, Rodman, Chilton, and I had stopped in London to prepare the way for such an expedition. There we met with representatives from fifteen potential troop contributor countries at a session the British Ministry of Defense hosted.

Washington was ready to support this U.K.-led effort, but the Pentagon had laid down strict conditions. First, the United States would not participate because it did not consider peacekeeping a fit role for American troops. Second, what the Bonn Agreement had called an "international security force" for Afghanistan should be renamed the "International Security Assistance Force" (ISAF), inserting the word *assistance* to eliminate any suggestion that international soldiers might themselves provide security for the Afghan population. As far as Washington was concerned, ensuring public safety was an Afghan responsibility. Given the absence of any Afghan national army or police, this stance effectively left security in the hands of local militia commanders. In Kabul's case, General Fahim was in charge.

Washington also wanted ISAF's geographic scope sharply circumscribed. The Bonn Agreement had called for international peacekeepers to be deployed initially to Kabul and then perhaps throughout the rest of Afghanistan. Washington adamantly opposed any such extension of ISAF. It insisted that even Bagram Air Base, which would become the main American operating hub in Afghanistan, just as it had been for the Soviet Union, should remain outside ISAF's area of operations.

After nearly a decade of organizing peacekeeping operations, I was accustomed to the American military's efforts to carefully delimit any task assigned to it. Resistance to "mission creep" had been one of the cardinal lessons the American defense establishment had drawn from the debacle in Somalia. This principle had been applied in designing the operations in Haiti, Bosnia, and Kosovo. In each of those instances, however, the American military planners' natural, even commendable, conservatism had been countered by the civilian leadership's insistence that the military help meet minimal mission requirements, the most essential of which was establishing a secure environment. Washington's setting geographical limits on ISAF was my first exposure to a mind-set that excluded local security as a post-conflict mission for U.S. forces.

The idea that Afghans could adequately secure their country after a twenty-three-year civil war struck me as naive and irresponsible. The limited ISAF mission Washington and London designed would be sufficient to achieve my immediate objective of installing a new government in Kabul, however. The city was peaceful. We had not heard any reports of large-scale looting or reprisals. A small, symbolic presence of international troops would provide the added element of reassurance needed to lure émigré opposition leaders back to their national capital. After that, we would see.

Before leaving London I had met with Maj. Gen. John McColl, the officer tentatively slated to command this international force. Prime Minister Blair had not yet committed Britain to assuming this role, and we understood the U.K. military was unenthusiastic, but Robert Cooper assured me that the prime minister would make the necessary decision within the next few days. McColl was on his way to Kabul to get the lay of the land and work out arrangements for the U.K. forces' arrival.

My first order of business in Kabul was to meet Hamid Karzai. Since 9/11, telephone calls to me aside, his only contacts with the U.S. government had been with the CIA officers who had supported his insurrection and with the Army Special Forces team that had subsequently joined them. Now that Karzai was transitioning from insurgent chieftain to head of state, the agency was eager to transfer liaison responsibility to the State Department. I was equally anxious to meet the person in whom so many hopes were now invested.

President Rabbani had thoughtfully made a wing of the presidential palace available to Karzai. Accompanied by Karp and Mudd, I visited the palace, a sprawling collection of low-lying brick and stone buildings behind several high walls. Karzai received us in a comfortable sitting room strewn with oriental carpets. He thanked me warmly for the support the United States had provided him to date. Within minutes I clearly saw why so many governments, which had agreed on little else, had seen this man as a good choice to lead Afghanistan's next government. Karzai was a good-looking individual, with strong, regular features. Speaking in easy, well-modulated tones, he established a quick rapport and exuded good will and candor.

Kandahar had fallen to insurgent forces shortly after our last phone conversation, freeing Karzai to come to Kabul and prepare for his new role. He told me of his arrival the previous evening on a U.S. Air Force transport. Defense Minister Fahim and an honor guard of Northern Alliance troops had greeted him when he debarked. After a few moments, when no one else got off the plane, a puzzled Fahim had asked him, "Where are your men?"

"You are my men," Karzai had responded, pointing to the phalanx of Northern Alliance soldiers drawn up behind Fahim. Karzai's decision not to bring along a contingent of Pashtun militia for his own protection was a significant gesture, for he avoided introducing another competing armed element within the city. It also exhibited considerable courage, for Fahim and Karzai were not strangers. Both had served together in an earlier, pre-Taliban government under Ahmed Shah Massoud. Fahim had headed the intelligence service while Karzai had been the deputy foreign minister. Tipped that Karzai was plotting against the government on behalf of Pakistani intelligence, Fahim had ordered his arrest and removal to an interrogation center not far from the presidential palace. There Fahim's men had worked on Karzai for several hours. When another contending warlord's forces lobbed mortar rounds, their blasts interrupted Karzai's questioning. He escaped in the ensuing confusion, bruised and bloodied from the encounter, and fled Kabul that same night. He had now returned, only to be greeted by the same man from whose custody he had fled seven years earlier.

Ready as Karzai might be to place his personal safety in Fahim's hands, he knew that other returning émigré leaders would be less trusting. Karzai therefore emphasized to me the importance of ISAF elements arriving in time for his inauguration the following week. He also asked whether international troops could be dispatched to the other major Afghan population centers. Peace was fragile throughout the country, not just in Kabul, he stressed. I explained that Washington was opposed to any such deployment. I suggested he raise the matter with Rumsfeld, who would be visiting Afghanistan the following day.

THE NEXT MORNING I returned to the palace to meet with Rabbani. On arrival I was shown into a large room occupied by several dozen robed and bearded figures arranged on couches and divans. Everyone wore several layers of clothes, which was the norm, as few buildings in Kabul had any heat. I was seated amid this throng and invited to say a few words. Shortly thereafter the meeting broke up, and Rabbani invited me to join him in a smaller nearby room. I never did find out whether I had interrupted a gathering called for another purpose or one assembled to greet me.

In our private meeting Rabbani was surprisingly warm and gracious. Having spent much of the past month maneuvering him out of office, I had expected to encounter at least some sign of resentment on his part. His remarks, however, were entirely constructive. He said he was making Karzai comfortable in the palace and would participate in his inauguration the following week. He also spoke of the need for peace and reconciliation. I promised continuous American engagement and support for his country's reconstruction. I left our meeting considerably reassured.

Abdullah and Qanooni were equally encouraging when I called at their respective ministries. Everything was in hand for the December 22 inauguration. It was shaping up to be quite an event, as they expected a host of visiting dignitaries and notables from all over Afghanistan, including all the principal warlords. Getting everyone in and out of town safely, ensuring the security of the site and its surroundings, arranging for live media coverage, and organizing the ceremony itself would put quite a strain on the capacity of Rabbani's government, which had only retaken its capital a couple of weeks earlier and would cease to exist on the day in question. Other than organizing air traffic at Bagram, the U.S. government could offer little in the way of logistical help.

The new government was the product of many factions and many external forces, but its inauguration was entirely the work of the three holdover ministers: Abdullah, who saw to the many foreign visitors' needs; Qanooni, who organized the event itself; and Fahim, who secured the city and its environs. With luck, an advance contingent of the international security force would arrive a day or two before the ceremony and provide at least symbolic reassurance, but all practical arrangements, including those for security, were in these three Afghans' hands.

In our respective meetings, Abdullah and Qanooni had both confided that they were thinking of forming a political party with Karzai that could transcend ethnic lines. I mentioned this possibility to Karzai at our next meeting. He seemed pleased and flattered but was also somewhat cautious. Political parties had a bad reputation in Afghanistan, and he felt it might be best if the country's new leader remained above the partisan fray. In the end he ultimately chose not to align himself with any faction.

GENERAL MCCOLL, the prospective ISAF commander, had flown in from London shortly after my team had arrived. We met at the British Embassy, where he recounted the difficulties he was encountering in pinning Defense Minister Fahim down about the arrangements necessary for deploying the ISAF's force. McColl said he would work the issue a bit longer, but he might need my assistance. Only American views, he noted resignedly, carried any real weight with the new Afghan leadership.

ARRIVING A DAY or two before I had, Brahimi and his staff had occupied a modern villa that was in somewhat better shape than most of the houses or offices I had seen. When we met, like Karzai, he was anxious for the ISAF troops to begin deploying. Brahimi also wanted them to operate beyond Kabul.

Later that afternoon, I drove back out to Bagram to greet Rumsfeld's plane. The secretary would be staying in Afghanistan only a few hours. Karzai and Fahim were also going out to meet with him. We all gathered in the large, cold ruin of a hangar. On debarking, the secretary took me aside and asked what to expect from his Afghan interlocutors.

"They will ask that ISAF be deployed beyond Kabul. They also want detachments sent to the other major population centers," I said.

"How many men would that take?" he asked skeptically.

"The British believe a force of five thousand would be adequate to secure Kabul. Given that the next four or five cities are all considerably smaller, perhaps another twenty thousand men might suffice," I suggested.

Rumsfeld did not pursue the matter, but his manner indicated his displeasure at the notion. He asked a few more unrelated questions and then drifted off to consult with his staff. Shortly thereafter, I left for Kabul. Night was falling, and my security detail insisted that we not chance our return after dark.

FOR THE NEXT several days, life became somewhat routine. Before dawn each morning those of us residing in the bunker began queuing up to use the single toilet, sink, and shower. Shortly after sunrise, one of our Afghan staffers would arrive with warm loaves of flat unleavened bread that had been cooked over open fires. Lunch and dinner consisted of the same, along with grilled kebabs. This repast was delicious the first few times, but it began to pall after several days. Following breakfast I would send out messengers to arrange meetings with various local luminaries. We spent much time waiting between encounters.

The outside temperature hovered slightly above freezing in the daytime. Everyone wore four or five layers of clothing. Rooms in a few places, such as the Presidential Palace, might enjoy a space heater, allowing us to shed our top layers. One day I was scheduled to film an interview at Kabul's InterContinental Hotel. Recalling the incongruous luxury of Tashkent's hotel,

I wondered whether a similar oasis of cosmopolitan ease might have survived twenty years of civil war. Perhaps it even had a restaurant that offered something besides kebabs. To my deep disappointment, I found Kabul's finest hostelry as devoid of amenities as the rest of the city. Guests wandered around a darkened and battered lobby in their overcoats. The restaurant was closed.

On December 16 we organized a ceremony to formally reopen the U.S. Embassy. Under the watchful gaze of marines manning sandbagged machine gun nests on the roof, numerous dignitaries and journalists assembled. Also in attendance were a dozen or so of the Afghan employees who had maintained and safeguarded the embassy compound over the intervening thirteen years. Members of the small diplomatic corps were present, as were the Afghan interior and defense ministers, Qanooni and Fahim. The day was heavily overcast, and a cold, light rain fell.

The marines guarding the compound also provided a color guard. As "The Star-Spangled Banner" rang out from a portable boom box, they were able to raise the very flag that had been lowered in 1989, when the last American diplomat had departed. On arrival, they had found an American flag in a locked vault in the embassy's basement. Sgt. James M. Blake, the noncommissioned officer then in charge of the marine security detachment, had attached a handwritten note to it: "Take care of the flag. For those of us here it means a lot. For those of you yet to enter Kabul, it could mean a lot to you. Semper Fi. We Kabul Marines endured, as I am sure you will."

I had invited Col. John Mulholland, the Special Forces commander who had greeted me at Bagram on November 16, to open the ceremonies. I followed his remarks with a brief statement pledging that the United States would stay engaged in Afghanistan and expressing support for the newly emerging Afghan regime.

"With the reopening of the United States Mission in Kabul today, America has resumed its diplomatic, economic, and political engagement with this country. We're here, and we're here to stay," I vowed. I acknowledged the United States and much of the rest of the world had ignored Afghanistan since the Soviets' withdrawal in 1989. On September 11 America paid the price for that neglect, but Afghanistan had been paying it for thirteen years.

"Afghan factions and Afghanistan's neighbors pursued their own narrow agendas without reference to the broader interests of the Afghan people. The new Afghan government will be led by a new generation of leaders who now have a historic opportunity to take Afghanistan into a new era."

As I spoke, the oldest and most senior of our Afghan employees translated my remarks one sentence at a time. This elderly gentleman had spent much of the past decade in prison for his loyalty to the United States.

Also in the audience was General McColl. As our guests assembled he had taken me aside to brief me on his negotiations with Fahim, which were not going well. Fahim wanted to limit both the overall size of the ISAF force and the scope of its activities. He was insisting that ISAF could patrol only in company with his own men, which would effectively allow him to determine where and when ISAF units operated.

When the ceremony was over I asked Fahim and Qanooni to join McColl and me for a few minutes. I wanted Qanooni involved because he had negotiated and signed the agreement calling for ISAF's deployment. We found a usable room inside the chancellery and pulled up chairs around a battered table. While Fahim and Qanooni were unaccompanied, McColl and I each had substantial entourages that soon filled the room to overflowing. Someone produced a map of Kabul, and another passed around a plate of pistachio cookies.

Fahim and Qanooni did not betray any discomfort at being outnumbered. I led the way through the outstanding issues, first asking McColl to make his case and then looking to the Afghans to respond. We were soon able to dispose of all but one matter. Fahim agreed that the ISAF's contingent would number around five thousand soldiers who would be free to patrol independently, although they would normally try to do so in the company of Afghan police. The only issue on which Fahim would not budge was his refusal to withdraw his own soldiers from the city once ISAF arrived.

I noted that the Bonn Agreement specified that its signatories "pledge to withdraw all military units from Kabul." I looked to Qanooni, one of those signatories, for confirmation. For the first time in our by then fairly extensive relationship, he did not give me an adequate response. He neither disputed the obligation nor acknowledged it. Clearly on this issue he felt unable to overrule his military colleague.

As I pressed him, Fahim explained that in his view, the language in the Bonn Agreement meant only that his troops would stay off the capital's streets, not that they would leave their caserns, some of which had housed the Afghan army for longer than a millennium. "You do not seriously intend that we would abandon the Bala Hissar," Fahim protested, referring to the city's historic citadel.

We seemed at in impasse. I had visions of the entire Bonn Agreement unraveling. If Fahim refused to withdraw, the British might refuse to deploy. Many émigré members of the new government might then refuse to take up their new positions. McColl, however, demonstrated both pragmatism and decisiveness. Seeing that I had pushed Fahim as far as he was likely to go, the general intervened. He said that he could live with Afghan soldiers remaining in their barracks, leaving the Afghan police and ISAF to patrol the streets. I concluded the meeting on this basis, still a bit worried about the reaction of the other Afghan factions but greatly relieved that we had not had a complete procedural breakdown while getting ISAF on the ground.

I have always been grateful to McColl for the cool judgment he displayed on this occasion. Although the outcome was inconsistent with a strict reading of the Bonn Agreement, Fahim's interpretation was just plausible enough to pass muster. McColl understood that his small force could do its job only with Fahim's cooperation and recognized that throwing thousands of Afghan troops out of their barracks at the onset of winter was not likely to secure that aid. Thus Fahim's troops stayed in their garrisons and had no serious confrontations with ISAF. Before McColl left later that day for London, he assured me that he would show up the following week with the lead element of his force.

FOLLOWING the embassy's opening I departed Kabul for brief visits to New Delhi and Islamabad. The trip gave me an opportunity to thank both governments for their cooperation in Bonn. I left most of my team behind. Karp was eager to spend more time exploring Kabul, and Mudd had work to do with the local agency representatives. Rodman and Chilton, assured that planning for ISAF was on track, had already headed back to Washington. Thus Gill and I boarded our familiar C-17 for the flight to Islamabad.

We arrived in the midst of a crisis in Indo-Pakistani relations. Five days earlier Kashmiri militants had attacked the Indian Parliament while that body was in full session, with the prime minister and his entire cabinet in attendance. Seven people were killed in an hour-long firefight. The Indian government saw Pakistani complicity in this attack and demanded that Islamabad allow the Indian authorities to conduct an investigation inside Pakistan. The Pakistanis predictably rejected this request, telling New Delhi, somewhat implausibly, that they would conduct their own inquiry. With Indian and Pakistani forces mobilizing, military action seemed increasingly likely. Both countries had acquired nuclear weapons during the past decade, making the confrontation particularly dangerous.

My arrival in Islamabad also coincided with the celebration of Eid, the major Muslim religious holiday marking the end of Ramadan. Foreign Secretary Inam ul-Haq returned from leave to host a lunch in my honor, a thoughtful gesture on a day normally spent with one's family. Whether it was the festive occasion or intervening events, Haq seemed much more relaxed about developments in Afghanistan than he and his colleagues had been on my last visit.

On the way back to the airport I stopped by the Anglo-American press center to give a briefing. Afghanistan was still comparatively inaccessible, and many journalists continued to cover the war from neighboring Pakistan. I expressed confidence that ISAF would soon be on the ground, said that Kabul was quiet, and predicted that Karzai's inauguration would take place on schedule.

Late that evening we arrived in New Delhi, where I was taken to Ambassador Blackwill's home. The same architect who had designed the Kennedy Center in Washington had also done both the embassy and the ambassador's residence. While these buildings shared the same monumental look, those in India were now a bit shabby. Security was less of a concern in New Delhi than it had been in Kabul and Islamabad. I found it a relief to move freely around the city for the next thirty-six hours without unarmored vehicles or a security detail.

Blackwill had arranged a busy schedule that included calls on the foreign minister and the prime minister's national security adviser. In both meetings much of our conversation centered on the current confrontation with Pakistan. The Indians made a strong case regarding Pakistani complicity. Blackwill listened sympathetically, seeking to establish a foundation of trust upon which the United States could subsequently build to defuse the conflict. Privately he worried that the Indians would retaliate militarily against Pakistan.

On my issues the Indians were congratulatory, pleased with the level of cooperation Ambassador Lambha and I had achieved in Bonn, and eager to assist the new Afghan regime. This stance created something of a dilemma. In Bonn, Lambha had been careful not to increase Pakistani paranoia or exacerbate Islamabad's quite accurate perception of having suffered a major geopolitical setback. In my meetings with the foreign minister and national security adviser, I praised the discretion and tact Lambha had displayed. Clearly, however, India now wanted a larger role in Afghanistan, one that was bound to make Pakistan uncomfortable. I did my best to temper this expectation without rebuffing my hosts' interest altogether.

Over lunch with Lambha I was more candid and expressed my concerns about the effect that Indo-Pakistani competition could have on Afghanistan. He acknowledged the problem and promised that his government would proceed cautiously. I could see though that pressure for a more substantial Indian presence was building.

Gill and I left New Delhi late in the afternoon with the intention of arriving at Bagram Air Base shortly before dawn. American aircraft would only land and take off from Bagram in the dark to reduce their vulnerability to ground fire. Embassy vehicles, meanwhile, would only traverse the road from Bagram to Kabul in the daytime.

Until the last moment we did not know whether we would receive clearance to overfly Pakistan. All air traffic between the two countries had been suspended, and both militaries were on high alert. I took some comfort in the thought that neither side was likely to mistake a C-17 for anything other than an American plane. As we approached our destination, the pilot invited me up to the cockpit to observe the landing, not that I could actually see anything. The sky was overcast, and not a single light flickered above or below us. The entire country was without electricity, and the population had long since doused their oil lanterns and gone to bed. Even Kabul, somewhere out in the distance, showed no glimmer whatsoever. More alarming, no lights demarcated the airfield. It was a security measure, the pilot explained, and we would land on a completely darkened field. He and his copilot put on night vision goggles. He assured me that his crew was one of a dozen or so in the entire U.S. Air Force trained and rated to land a C-17 in the pitch black of night. None of the crew appeared older than twenty-five years of age, but they all seemed to know what they were doing. If they didn't, I reflected, I would never know.

Bagram sits in a bowl surrounded by mountains. The pilot advised me that we would corkscrew down, descending as quickly as possible to minimize the exposure to any enemy with a handheld antiaircraft missile. Only a few minutes into our descent I heard a calm, well-modulated female voice announce, "Incoming missile." Then the voice cited the vector on which it was approaching. In response, everyone on the flight deck turned to look in the indicated direction. This warning occurred several times during our descent. The pilot and crew did not appear unduly alarmed.

"Don't worry," the pilot urged. "The missile attack alarm is quite sensitive and often reports false positives." As we spiraled downward in the dark, I sought to reassure myself by reflecting on the undoubted excellence of U.S. Air Force personnel, training, and equipment.

Once on the ground, we were escorted to the tent housing the sleeping soldiers, coffee urn, and picnic tables. We helped ourselves to coffee and sat around the tables, listening to the gentle snores from those behind the curtain. After a while a Green Beret sergeant just back from patrol joined us. He chatted with us briefly. Soon he too went to bed, and at first light we set out for Kabul.

INAUGURATION DAY, December 22, dawned cold and clear. Gen. Tommy Franks had flown in for the ceremony, and a helicopter brought him to the embassy. A dozen of us stood and looked up as the aircraft descended, only to be driven to the nearest shelter by a thick cloud of dust and debris raised by the swirling rotors.

To my surprise, Franks's wife, Cathy, accompanied him. Afghanistan was still an active war zone. It would be years before the State Department permitted dependents to visit, even briefly. Cathy would almost certainly be the only wife among the several thousand guests attending the inauguration. In his memoir, Franks notes with a certain air of bravado that he carried a concealed weapon throughout the inauguration ceremonies. Cathy proved a pleasant and undemanding companion throughout the day.

We drove to the inaugural site in several of the embassy's armored Suburbans. On the way I briefed Franks on a late-breaking news item. The media was reporting that an American aircraft had attacked a convoy of tribal elders on their way to Karzai's swearing in, killing a large number of them. Franks and his accompanying staffers said that they had not heard anything about this incident.

As we neared our destination, Franks said he preferred to avoid the press and asked me to handle any inquiries. Getting out of our vehicle, however, he immediately headed for a gaggle of reporters and held an impromptu press conference. Seeing my puzzled expression, Cathy explained that President Bush had asked her husband to make himself more available to the media.

I went over and listened to the exchange. As I approached, the press asked Franks about the reported attack on the convoy of inauguration guests en route to Kabul. The general denied categorically that any such incident had taken place.

I was somewhat taken aback by the confidence with which Franks denied this story. I was also, however, relieved that he had effectively squelched a report that could otherwise have cast a serious pall over the day's events. Thanks to Franks's categorical denial, press coverage of the inauguration did not heavily feature reports of the misguided attack. Of course the story gained new legs when the U.S. military spokesman confirmed the attack several days later. An American aircraft had indeed bombed the convoy in question under the mistaken impression that the vehicles' occupants were Taliban members. By then the media focus on Afghanistan had diminished a bit, and the inauguration had been duly recorded.

Over the next few months, I saw a few more examples of this "deny first, investigate later" response to allegations of misguided attacks by U.S. forces. After further similar reports were confirmed, however, U.S. military spokesmen began to adopt the more prudent "we're checking on it" reaction.

After Franks's impromptu press conference, our party left the parking lot and its confusion of arriving motorcades and entered the large auditorium, where several thousand people had assembled. The hall was decorated with large portraits of the assassinated Northern Alliance military commander, Ahmed Shah Massoud. Although this occasion was a day of national unity, its Panjshiri organizers—Qanooni, Abdullah, and Fahim—also took the opportunity to pay tribute to their martyred leader. The government taking office this day did, in fact, owe a good deal to Massoud's conviction that the Northern Alliance would need to share power with a wider circle of Pashtun figures if Afghanistan was to avoid further civil war.

Our party numbered about a dozen. I had arranged for several of our Afghan employees to be included so that they could provide us a running translation of the day's events, which would be conducted mostly in Dari or Pashto. Unfortunately, Franks, his wife, and I were separated from the rest of our entourage and shown to a place of honor in the front row. We thus spent the next several hours not knowing what was being said.

Rather amazingly, the event started on schedule. The Afghans had managed to bring in thousands of celebrants from all over the country and indeed from all over the world. Iranian foreign minister Kharrazi swept in, with Ismail Khan, another Tajik warlord and master of Herat, in his wake. Belgium's foreign minister plopped down beside me. Representatives of Pakistan, India, and Russia, countries that had helped tear Afghanistan apart for the past twenty years, were all in attendance.

The ceremony opened with readings from the Koran and the singing of the national anthem. Brahimi then spoke. He addressed us in English; consequently, he was one of the few speakers most of the foreign observers could understand. Iranian foreign minister Kharrazi and Belgian foreign minister Louis Michel, on behalf of the European Commission, also spoke. Rabbani came next. His dignified presence and positive manner underscored the peaceful and cooperative nature of this transfer of power.

Finally we heard from Karzai, who was attired for the first time in what would become his trademark costume—a stylish mix of Pashtun, Uzbek, and Tajik traditional dress topped off with a particularly colorful embroidered cape. The symbolism was impressive. Formally, Karzai was no more than the chairman of an Interim Administration intended to last only six months. On this day, however, the Afghans had invested him with all the authority of a head of state. He represented the hopes of their nation, a country sick to death of war.

Once Karzai and the ministers of the Interim Administration had taken their oaths of office, the senior guests were led back to their motorcades, another impressive feat of organization, and driven to the Presidential Palace for lunch. Franks and I were seated at far ends of the table, again without interpreters, so conversation around us lagged. At our departure, both Ismail Khan and Abdul Rashid Dostum came over, introduced themselves, and pledged their continued cooperation.

Dostum greeted Franks, "Who do you want me to fight next?"

While Franks and I were at the palace, a U.S. Army helicopter flying over Kabul had reported ground fire aimed in its direction. We decided therefore to drive the general and Mrs. Franks to Bagram in our embassy vehicles. Along the full distance of the now-familiar road from Kabul to the air base Afghan soldiers stood at hundred-yard intervals. A temporary bridge had been installed over the stream that we had forded on our last several trips. Our Suburbans were wider than the bridge, so we still had to ford the stream, which was rising alarmingly. The detour around the road's mined area had also been removed, one hoped after first clearing the mines.

As we bumped along, the topic of conversation turned to the difficulties Franks had in getting his female soldiers in Saudi Arabia to respect local customs and, in particular, to obey his order that they wear head scarves whenever they ventured off the base. One female officer had protested the directive and was facing court-martial as a result. The matter had reached the press and clearly irked the general. Apparently expecting sympathy for his stance, Franks turned to an accompanying embassy officer, a woman.

"Wouldn't the State Department require the same of its female personnel?" he asked.

She replied quietly that it would not.

At Bagram planes awaited us. Tommy and Cathy Franks flew off to celebrate Christmas with the troops at other Middle East locations. My team and I headed back to Washington, eager to reach home in time for the holiday.

9

NATION-BUILDING

I ARRIVED IN WASHINGTON exhausted. The flights had been comfortable enough but interminable. The U.S. Air Force had taken us to Tashkent, where Karp and I boarded commercial jets to Istanbul, New York, and finally Washington. We had traveled with the sun, and the flight took place in seemingly endless daylight.

As far as I was concerned, my Afghan interlude was at an end. I had been asked to forge the opposition into a government that could succeed the Taliban. That mission was now accomplished. I knew that harder tasks lay ahead for those who would try to put in place the building blocks of a viable state, one capable of securing its people and controlling its territory without a foreign troop presence. Repeated experience told me that the exhilaration of liberation would soon be replaced by an even deeper sense of frustration at the intractable problems associated with nation-building.

Before traveling to Kabul for Karzai's inauguration I had taken myself out of the running for that assignment. I had overseen our country's last four post-conflict reconstruction efforts and was ready to let someone else take up the task. I thus recommended Khalilzad for the post of American ambassador in Kabul. From our time together in Bonn I saw that he had an excellent rapport with all the main Afghan leaders. His policy judgments were sound, and he also enjoyed a better relationship with Rumsfeld's Pentagon than I was ever likely to achieve.

This idea initially met with a reserved response all around. Powell preferred to put another Foreign Service officer in the position, someone who would be steady, reliable, and closely tied to his department. Rice was reluctant to lose Khalilzad, whose responsibilities on her staff encompassed the entire Middle East. Khalilzad, for his part, was unsure where Afghanistan would rank among the administration's many competing priorities. It was not till some eighteen months later he went out as ambassador, and then he went only after President Bush had personally him asked to accept the assignment. Khalilzad managed to secure a hefty increase in U.S. assistance in conjunction with his assignment and served with distinction in Kabul for nearly two years before moving on to an even more daunting position in Baghdad.

On my return from Kabul, Armitage asked to see me. Rice and Powell wanted me to assume oversight responsibility for Afghan reconstruction, if not in Kabul, then in Washington. They understood that I was planning on leaving the government and were not asking that I postpone that move, only that I run the interagency process for as long as I remained. On the understanding that this assignment would not last more than a few months, I agreed.

I asked Armitage what would be expected of me. He explained that Rice wanted to transfer responsibility for interagency coordination on all things Afghan from the National Security Council staff, where it had resided since 9/11, to the State Department. I would accordingly both run State Department operations and chair a multiagency committee to oversee the work of other departments. In this capacity, I would have access to Powell and Armitage whenever necessary, but I would report formally to Christina Rocca, the assistant secretary for South Asia.

I had serious doubts about the workability of this arrangement. Only the White House could adjudicate differences between the State Department and DOD, of which there were bound to be many. Assigning State the lead for an activity where most of the assets were bound to come from DOD was in my view an abdication of White House responsibility, a sign that Afghanistan was already slipping in the administration's list of priorities.

I also did not believe that the position being created would carry adequate weight throughout the rest of the government, not to speak of the rest of the world, if it were located within the Bureau of South Asian Affairs, the smallest, weakest, and least prestigious of the State Department's six regional subdivisions. This arrangement was an indication that State, like the NSC, was returning Afghanistan to the category of "business as usual."

The move reflected Powell's orderly approach to organization and delegation of authority. During the Clinton administration a profusion of special envoys had been created to deal with various hot spots, each nominally working directly for the secretary of state and sometimes even for the president. I had held several of these assignments. Powell, on assuming charge of the department, had abolished all these positions and returned their functions to the respective regional bureaus. By the time he had made that decision, I was heading the largest and most powerful of those bureaus, that responsible for relations with Europe, so his decision had suited my immediate bureaucratic interests just fine. I had however not delegated responsibility for keeping Bosnia and Kosovo on track; rather, I had focused largely on these issues and delegated others to my subordinates. Now, a year later, I was being asked to oversee a much larger and more difficult reconstruction effort from a much less powerful position.

Had I been planning on a longer tenure I would have argued that responsibility for interagency coordination should remain with the National Security Council staff and that the new Afghan coordinator at the State Department should report, at least nominally, to the secretary. As it was, I saw little point in insisting on prerogatives that I did not intend to exercise for more than a few months. All I asked, therefore, was that I be given the authority to recruit a small staff and to allocate the assistance that was committed to Afghanistan. Armitage agreed to both, although in the end he encountered difficulty delivering either during my tenure.

EARLY IN THE NEW YEAR I set off for Tokyo to join Colin Powell for an international conference that had been called to raise money for Afghanistan's reconstruction. The gathering provided a forum for several dozen foreign and finance ministers to announce the amounts their governments were prepared to commit for that purpose. Each of these officials felt compelled to make a statement, which ran a minimum of at least ten to fifteen minutes. With forty to fifty countries represented, it meant several days of speechifying. Other than the speaker, relatively junior officials sat behind most of the national placards. The other ministers held bilateral discussions in adjoining rooms, worked their cell phones, or went shopping.

The meeting succeeded in securing pledges for some $5 billion in assistance, and much of the concluding rhetoric was self-congratulatory. While we secured a good deal of money, I pointed out to Powell that on a per capita basis, this amount represented substantially less than similar conferences had raised for Bosnia or Kosovo, both of which were much richer societies that had suffered less devastation. Powell let this comment pass with an impatient shrug. He could not pledge what he did not have, and the administration was not planning to make a new request to Congress.

Of the $5 billion raised in Tokyo, the United States pledged only $290 million, little more than 5 percent of the total. To be fair, the American pledge was for a single year, while the promised aid from other countries was often intended to be spread over a longer period. Powell's pledge represented money Congress had allocated for Afghanistan some months earlier, at which point the funds had been intended for humanitarian assistance to refugees and those directly impacted by what was then anticipated to be a protracted military campaign. In other words, having liberated Afghanistan, the United States was proposing to provide Afghans the same amount of assistance they would have received had they remained under the Taliban.

The United States has the world's largest economy, with a gross domestic product representing well over 20 percent of the global total. America's pledges to the reconstruction of Bosnia and Kosovo had been commensurate with that ability to pay, representing about a fifth of the overall reconstruction monies raised. The effect of American initial parsimony with respect to Afghanistan was twofold. First, the paltry American contribution reduced Washington's ability to exercise a strong leadership role in overseeing reconstruction. Second, it led other governments to lowball their contributions as well. While $5 billion may sound like a great deal, it is less so when one divides it among more than 25 million impoverished Afghans. In their first year of reconstruction, Bosnians received sixteen times more international assistance than did Afghans. Kosovars received eight times more.

Among the pledges made in Tokyo that exceeded the American offer was that of Iran. The revolutionary regime in Tehran promised $540 million in assistance to its neighbor. Nearly twice the U.S. commitment, Tehran's pledge was very impressive for any still developing country.

SEVERAL OF THE IRANIAN diplomats who had attended the Bonn Conference showed up again in Tokyo. Emerging from a larger gathering, one of them took me aside to reaffirm his government's desire to continue to cooperate on Afghanistan. I agreed that this stance would be desirable but warned that Iranian behavior in other areas represented an obstacle to cooperation.

"We would like to discuss the other issues with you also," he replied.

"My brief only extends to Afghanistan," I cautioned.

"We know that. We would like to work on these other issues with the appropriate people in your government."

"The *Karine A* incident was not helpful," I said, referring to a Palestinian ship intercepted a few days earlier by the Israeli Navy on its way to Gaza. The ship was loaded with several tons of weapons of Iranian origin.

"We too are concerned about this," the Iranian diplomat said. "President Mohammad Khatami met earlier this week with the National Security Council. He asked whether any of the agency heads present knew anything about this shipment. All of them denied any knowledge. If your government has information on the origin of these weapons that it can provide us that would be most helpful."

Unbeknownst to me at the time, the Iranians had approached Treasury Secretary Paul O'Neill, who also attended the same Tokyo meeting. His interlocutor was Mrs. Sadako Ogata, the former United Nations High Commissioner for Refugees. She asked to see O'Neill in order to pass on a message from the Iranian government. Ogata told O'Neill that the Iranians wanted to open a dialogue with Washington covering all of the issues that divided the two countries.

On returning to Washington, O'Neill and I reported these conversations, he to Rice and to his cabinet-level colleagues and I to State's Middle Eastern Bureau. No one evinced any interest, but the Iranians received a very public response. One week later, in his State of the Union address, President Bush named Iran, along with Iraq and North Korea, as part of what he termed an "axis of evil." How archenemies like Iran and Iraq could form an axis, evil or otherwise, was never explained. His remarks raised the prospect of preemptive military action intended to halt these three states' acquisition of weapons of mass destruction. He did not mention whatsoever the helpful role Iran had played in enabling the American military victory in Afghanistan and in supporting American diplomacy in Bonn.

MY MAIN PURPOSE in Tokyo was to enlist donors' help in reforming the Afghan army, police, courts, and prisons. I knew rebuilding these security institutions would be key to establishing an environment in which refugees could safely return, commerce could resume, and economic and political reforms could begin to take hold. Rapid progress in rebuilding the Afghans' capacity to provide for public safety would be doubly important given the Bush administration's refusal to have American troops engage in peacekeeping and its resistance to having anyone else do so.

I spent my first couple of days in Tokyo meeting individually with representatives from those other governments that were likely to invest in Afghan security. It was always a hard sell. Most international donors prefer to support projects that tug their voters' heartstrings and have little potential for scandal. On the one hand, schools and hospitals were safe bets, and their funding consequently tends to be oversubscribed. On the other hand, armies and police could be abusive and judges corrupt. Jails were a particularly unattractive candidate for international assistance. Yet if these activities were not adequately funded, everything spent on economic, social, and political reform would ultimately be wasted as the war-torn society slipped back into conflict.

The international community's collective experience in the Balkans had some effect in overcoming these inhibitions. The World Bank, usually the biggest single source of development assistance, was still leery of getting involved in the security sector. Other international donors were coming around, however. In our conversations, the Germans indicated an interest in training the Afghan police, the French in training the army, the British in heading an antinarcotics effort, and the Italians in rebuilding the court system. Even the Japanese, long the most cautious of donors about involvement in such matters, indicated their interest in funding a program to disarm the Afghan militias.

The major regional powers were also keen to participate in this effort. Pakistan, India, and Iran each wanted to help rebuild the Afghan army and police force. Their offers presented a delicate challenge. On the one hand, these governments certainly could contribute to the effort. These countries, after all, had been training and equipping Afghan troops for the past couple of decades. In most respects, therefore, they were far better qualified than the United States or its European allies to train an Afghan force. On the other hand, the prospect of Pakistan, India, and Iran collaborating effectively in such an enterprise was low. Bringing these governments into the process would introduce their competition into the various Afghan institutions, as each government sought to use its training programs to recruit agents of influence and build up a local clientele. Western governments might do likewise, but their interests were less directly engaged and more mutually compatible.

At the same time, I did not want to turn down these major regional powers' offers entirely. Each government had provided valuable support to my efforts in Bonn. Sustaining their constructive engagement was essential to any effort to stabilize Afghanistan. I therefore made a point of continuing to consult with all of these governments.

Having laid the ground work, I chaired a meeting involving the several dozen countries interested in helping reform Afghanistan's security institutions. Brahimi sat to my left and Foreign Minister Abdullah to my right in order to emphasize that our effort also enjoyed the backing of both the United Nations and the new Afghan government. Each of us made a plea for assistance. I said that the United States was ready to take the lead in building a new Afghan army and that we hoped other governments would step up and accept similar responsibilities for other areas. As arranged, the Germans, Italians, British, and Japanese expressed interest in the specific areas mentioned. Subsequently the French offered to join the United States in training the new army. Predictably, no one volunteered to help rebuild the prisons.

The lead nation arrangement for managing Afghan reconstruction has since been much criticized and with good reason. No nation, including most notably the United States, made the effort necessary to get these institutions up and running. Neither were lead nations able to secure significant support for their programs from other donors, for few wanted to accept another government's oversight. Afghanistan would have been better served if we had assigned responsibility for organizing the international assistance effort to some new or existing multilateral organization, as had been done for Bosnia and Kosovo. Alternatively, the United States might have assumed the lead role in multiple sectors, as it had done in Haiti. The first option would have required a greater commitment to multilateralism than the Bush administration was then ready for and the second a greater U.S. commitment to nation-building.

But the fault did not entirely lie with the United States. The United Nations was also not interested in accepting responsibility for overseeing Afghanistan's economic development or reform of its security sector.

Don Rumsfeld's resistance to institutionalizing multilateral arrangements for nation-building derived from his failed attempt to withdraw American troops from Bosnia in 2001. Colin Powell had countered Rumsfeld's effort by arguing that the American commitment to Bosnia was part of a broader multilateral engagement that could only be terminated with NATO's agreement. Still chafing from this early bureaucratic setback, Rumsfeld was determined to avoid any similar entanglement with Afghanistan. Although by 2004 he would be keen to have NATO assume the burden of securing Afghanistan, in early 2002 he still regarded any such multilateral engagement as unnecessarily constraining.

Brahimi, for very different reasons, was reluctant to see the United Nations' role expanded. From his long association with that organization, he had a keen understanding of its limitations. He doubted its ability to adequately oversee either the security or economic aspects of the international community's activities in Afghanistan. Recognizing his own greatest strength—political development—he wanted to head a lean mission that would concentrate on implementing the steps toward full democratic and constitutional government laid out in the Bonn Agreement. He was content to advise and support others who might take the lead in the economic and security spheres. Like Rumsfeld but with different motives, Brahimi thus favored what was coming to be called the "low-profile, small-footprint approach" to nation-building.

One area where these men's minimalist visions clashed was with regard to peacekeeping. Brahimi wanted international troops to patrol Kabul and the other major population centers. Further, he wanted to gradually displace the warlords and disband their militias. He felt heavily armed, well-equipped Western troops under American or NATO command could better perform these security tasks than a more lightly equipped UN peacekeeping force.

By contrast, Rumsfeld's preference, which General Franks shared, was to continue to rely on the local warlords who controlled indigenous Afghan forces to hunt down the remaining al Qaeda and Taliban elements. U.S. troop levels would be kept to the absolute minimum necessary to stiffen cooperating Afghan units and go after high-value al Qaeda targets. Rumsfeld and Franks had gone along reluctantly with deploying international peacekeepers in Kabul, but they still objected to dispatching them elsewhere and opposed having American troops undertake this role.

The rationale for their opposition was based on several beliefs. First, the administration felt that the Afghans were world-renowned xenophobes who would resist any new foreign incursion, as they had the British in the nineteenth century and the Soviets in the twentieth century. Next, the administration believed that the U.S. military's proper function was to fight and win the nation's wars and not to escort children to school, as Condoleezza Rice had said when referring derisively to the American military's role in the Balkans. The administration also viewed peacekeeping as a failed concept, ineffective in halting conflict. Further, the Pentagon feared that any effort to extend ISAF to other parts of Afghanistan would strain American logistical resources, even if the troops involved were European, at a time when Washington was already looking to carry the war on terror to other theaters. And finally General Franks feared that international peacekeepers might clash with the local militias that the United States was counting on to help hunt down al Qaeda and Taliban remnants.

If the U.S. administration was unwilling to embark upon or even endorse a nationwide peacekeeping mission, it was equally uninterested in assuming a leadership role in the civil sphere. Doing so would have required that the United States take up the challenge of organizing police training, judicial reform, and prison reform; helping rebuild capacity within a nearly nonexistent Afghan government apparatus; and coordinating international development assistance. Washington had no plans for such engagements, and furthermore, it had not set aside any money to fund it.

In the weeks following the Tokyo conference I therefore worked to flesh out the lead nation arrangement while simultaneously pushing both the United States and the United Nations to do more. Four cochairs—Japan, the European Union, the World Bank, and Saudi Arabia—had run the Tokyo donors meeting. The Saudis had been added in the hopes of attracting donations from the Persian Gulf oil states. This unwieldy group of cochairs decided to continue to coordinate international support for Afghan economic development, while in Kabul, the World Bank and the Afghan government would establish and cochair another committee encompassing a larger collection of donors. These arrangements struck me as most unpromising. The four Tokyo cochairs would have a hard time agreeing on anything among themselves let alone impose discipline on the broader donor community. The World Bank would provide significant funding and good advice on economic development, but it would shy away from aid to soldiers, police, courts, or prisons. Finally, according leadership to the Afghan government was problematic. Had the Afghan government been capable of overseeing the implementation of international assistance, it would not have needed much of that aid in the first place. It was precisely because the Afghan government was flat on its back that a large-scale program of assistance was necessary.

In my view, the United States and the United Nations together should have guided the Afghan reconstruction effort and ensured that economic assistance flowed on a priority basis to those areas most likely to help stabilize the country. Both were reluctant to do so, however. Washington wanted others to fund the lion's share of economic aid; therefore, it could not make any claim to such overall leadership. When I suggested to Brahimi that rather than asking a World Bank representative, he should chair the committee in Kabul that would coordinate donor aid, he declined. Instead, he was content that one of his deputies should sit as a mere member of that committee.

The failure to include international police was another glaring gap in the Afghan reconstruction effort. In the 1990s, the United States had deployed a thousand American, French, Canadian, Caribbean, and Latin American police to augment Haiti's military peacekeepers. In Bosnia the United Nations had deployed nearly two thousand international policemen to supplement the efforts of sixty thousand NATO soldiers. In Kosovo the ratio of international police to military forces was raised further, with nearly five thousand UN-led international police operating alongside some fifty thousand NATO soldiers.

By the end of the 1990s the ratio of one international policeman for every ten soldiers had become the norm for most peacekeeping missions. The main function of the international police force was to train, monitor, and mentor local police. In circumstances where the indigenous police was non-existent or totally unreliable, the international police would also enforce the law. I asked Brahimi several times whether it would not make sense for the United Nations to deploy civilian police to Afghanistan, but he responded unenthusiastically. I could understand why. If Washington was opposed to sending international soldiers into the countryside, how could the United Nations seriously consider sending lightly armed police? Yet even if international police had been limited to Kabul, a five thousand–man ISAF force there could have justified a five hundred–person international police unit. This presence would have been a start toward ensuring security.

I ALSO PERSISTED in pressing the case for ISAF's geographic expansion. My ally in this effort was Robert Cooper of the British Cabinet Office. Cooper led a British delegation to Washington in late January for a review of Afghanistan's situation. We met at the State Department. On my side of the table were representatives from Rumsfeld's office, the Joint Chiefs, the CIA, and the various elements of my own department. Cooper's team was composed similarly.

The British briefed us on their progress in getting ISAF up and running. Happily, it was going well. Our discussion then turned to the security situation throughout the rest of the country. To the extent that these areas were under anyone's control, tribal leaders and local militia commanders ruled them. In the north those individuals were the same warlords that had made up the Northern Alliance, and in the south, smaller, less-organized bands, some of which had opposed the Taliban and others had collaborated with it, exercised their influence. Nominally, all these men were now loyal to Karzai.

Their more-structured units were also theoretically subordinated to Fahim's Ministry of Defense. The government in Kabul, however, had neither the money to pay these forces nor the practical means of exercising any authority over them. Each commander thus had to extract the necessary funds to feed, clothe, house, and pay his troops as best he could. This self-reliance forced them to exact roadblocks, tolls, and other forms of extortion. As time went on, they resorted to drug trafficking.

Already several of these armed bands were jockeying for control over territory and population and coming into conflict with each other as a result. Commanders regularly tried to entice the United States to come in on their side by charging that their rivals were collaborating with the Taliban. The most serious incidents took place in and around the northern town of Mazar-e-Sharif, where Uzbek troops under General Dostum and Tajiks under Mohammed Ata had rubbed up against one another, sometimes violently, as their leaders vied to dominate the city and its surroundings.

Cooper and I believed ISAF's expansion was urgent. Our military colleagues were opposed, mine vocally and Cooper's somewhat reservedly. Rumor had it that the chief of the U.K. Defence Staff had been strongly opposed to Britain taking on the ISAF mission. Prime Minister Blair had only dissuaded him from resigning in protest after promising that the United Kingdom's commitment there would be short lived.

At one point a British officer asked straight out whether the United States would support the deployment of peacekeepers outside Kabul.

"Yes," I responded, "the administration will support ISAF's expansion. The only question is whether it will do so before or after some disaster forces its hand."

My answer greatly annoyed my Pentagon colleagues, who were under orders to resist any deployments.

A few days later the British ambassador invited me to dinner with his boss, Foreign Secretary Jack Straw. The ambassador noted that both our governments were debating the issue of ISAF expansion, and he asked me to give Straw my view of it. I said that Karzai and Brahimi both wanted ISAF to be extended to the other Afghan cities. So, interesting enough, did many of the competing warlords, including Ismail Khan, Fahim, Atta, and Dostum. I advised that the Bush administration was against allowing American forces to be used in a peacekeeping role; therefore, if the job were to be done at all, the burden would fall largely on the European allies. Many European governments had been eager, in the aftermath of 9/11, for some military role in Afghanistan. Here was their chance.

Straw listened carefully and asked some insightful questions, but he gave no indication of his own view. Several weeks later, the Blair government announced that the United Kingdom would give up the leadership of ISAF by midyear. British troops would then join American forces in southern Afghanistan for operations designed to root out remaining Taliban and al Qaeda elements.

This shift in roles provided a clever means of reducing British military commitments in Afghanistan while appearing to do the opposite. British troops seemed to be trading a safe assignment in Kabul for real war fighting in the south. In fact, their commitment in the south lasted only a matter of weeks, at the end of which most British troops were withdrawn. But like the Americans, British soldiers would return in force years later, after the Taliban had reasserted itself.

AS THE DEBATE in Washington wore on, the media became aware of the ongoing dispute between the State and Defense departments. During a visit to Nellis Air Force Base, Rumsfeld referred to State Department proposals for expanding ISAF, making clear his own views were otherwise and leaving the impression that the issue had already been decided in his favor. Michael Gordon of the *New York Times* called me for a reaction. I said that the issue was still being discussed within the administration and that no decision had been reached. The next morning, on reading the article, Rice had one of her deputies, Gen. Wayne Downing, call me with a formal reprimand.

"I assume the secretary of defense is being similarly reprimanded," I responded rather sharply.

"Yes, of course," Downing replied weakly. His tone and manner suggested otherwise.

This minor incident illustrated several facets of life in the Bush administration. Any White House tries to screen internal debates from public scrutiny, but this administration was particularly neuralgic on the subject. Yet it was also unable or unwilling to exercise any real discipline concerning its defense secretary's public statements. So instead of remonstrating with him for putting out his version of the issue, it slapped me down for setting the record straight.

Eventually the matter came to a head. Rice called a meeting to decide whether to expand ISAF. In preparation for the meeting Elliott Abrams, who headed a directorate within the National Security Council, circulated a paper asserting that peacekeeping was, in fact, a failed concept, one that had been tried and found wanting throughout the 1990s. His assertions were completely counterfactual. By 2002 tens of millions of people in such places as Namibia, Cambodia, Mozambique, El Salvador, East Timor, Sierra Leone, Albania, Bosnia, Kosovo, and Macedonia were living at peace—and for the most part under freely elected governments—because UN, NATO, American, or European troops had come in, separated combatants, disarmed contending factions, rebuilt the country, held elections, installed new governments, and stayed around long enough to watch them take root. Such was the prevalent prejudice against nation-building within the Bush administration, however, that this ludicrously misleading paper went unchallenged.

We met in the White House Situation Room. Powell and I attended for the State Department, and Rice chaired. Others present included Rumsfeld and Tenet. With Powell and Rumsfeld at loggerheads, Tenet's input could be decisive. In theory, the CIA just provided intelligence and analysis, not policy advice, but Tenet's people had masterminded the just-concluded war. They were more knowledgeable about what was going on in Afghanistan than anyone at either the State or the Defense Department. Tenet confirmed that some skirmishing among commanders theoretically under Karzai's authority had occurred, and there was danger that this fighting could escalate.

Rumsfeld argued that it was pointless to consider expanding ISAF because there were no volunteers to man such an enlarged force. No government, he noted, had yet offered troops for the purpose. This point was true but somewhat disingenuous since no one had yet asked for volunteers. Moreover, no allied ministry of defense was going to proffer units for a mission the American secretary of defense opposed. And Rumsfeld had made his opposition to this enterprise well known. Public interest in Afghanistan was nevertheless still high throughout Europe. An active American effort to promote the expanded ISAF mission would likely draw support from a number of quarters.

After several inconclusive exchanges between Powell and Rumsfeld, Rice asked all the backbenchers to leave the room. Thus the principals could discuss the matter further in private.

After another fifteen minutes the meeting broke, and Powell emerged to fill me in on its result. In the end everyone had acknowledged that left to their own devices, Afghanistan's warlords were likely to resume fighting. Rumsfeld had remained adamant, however, against dispatching peacekeepers. As an alternative, he proposed that the American liaison teams already working with most of the major Afghan commanders use their influence to keep the peace among their charges. Powell and Rice had agreed. So we would see no call for international troops, no ISAF expansion, no additional forces, and no public security duties for American soldiers, but an effort would be made to tamp down any incipient conflict. While the United States would use its considerable influence to forestall fighting among them, Afghanistan's warlords would remain free to treat the civilian population as they wished.

I looked disappointed.

Powell shrugged, "It's the best I could do. Rumsfeld promised he would handle the problem. What more could I say?"

Again Powell had chosen not to challenge Rumsfeld on the latter's turf. Powell's responsibility was foreign policy, and while he might know more about defense than the secretary of defense, on those issues he was reluctant to engage him head-on.

SEVERAL DAYS later Steve Hadley chaired a follow-up meeting. When I asked whether we could all see the instruction that had been sent out to U.S. commanders pursuant to this agreement, Doug Feith, the DOD representative, immediately became very defensive. He maintained that sharing this sort of operational traffic outside military channels would be inappropriate. This contention was nonsense. In any previous administration a message of this broad import and general interest would be provided to the State Department, probably automatically and certainly on request. In Rumsfeld's Pentagon, however, no subordinate made any decision, no matter how trivial, without reference to the boss, and the boss was seldom inclined to share.

Hadley, nevertheless, agreed with me and directed Feith to share the message. He never did. For several weeks I pressed for a copy, with Hadley's support, but to no avail. I began to suspect that the instruction had never been sent; rather, in all likelihood, Rumsfeld had filled Franks in on the results of the principals' meeting orally. This communication would have allowed him to put a cast on the matter that he might not have wished to share with the White House and the State Department.

In any case, one way or another, the word did go out, and American officers in the field did intervene effectively on several occasions to defuse confrontations among local Afghan commanders. Rumsfeld's compromise thus achieved the immediate purpose of forestalling a renewal of civil war; however, it did not improve security for the general population or for the international community. Armed bands, some purely criminal, some loosely associated with the government, arbitrarily interfered with the transportation of goods, services, and people. Responsible for the safety of American civilian officials, the State Department forbade their travel outside Kabul without an armed escort, but that agency, as a practical matter, was unable to provide it. Consequently, American officials were confined to the capital. Other national and international agencies followed suit, resulting in a debilitating limitation on reconstruction outside the capital. The security situation also deterred merchants and private investors from traveling freely, thus slowing the country's economic growth. Drug trafficking was the notable exception. The traffickers, alone among entrepreneurs, had enough money to buy protection from the local warlords or to hire a militia of their own.

Following the decision not to expand ISAF, the issue of how to promote economic and political reform in Afghanistan was remanded to the interagency group under my chairmanship. To get State Department and USAID officers out of Kabul and into the provinces, I proposed that DOD allow American civilian officials to live and work within military compounds in the areas where U.S. troops were active. Both Defense Department and USAID representatives responded dubiously. DOD didn't think protecting U.S. government civilians was part of its job, and USAID was used to relying on the State Department for its people's security. Nevertheless, at my level, everyone recognized that allowing civilians access to military compounds was the only way U.S. officials would ever get out of Kabul. Both DOD and USAID representatives agreed, therefore, to take the issue back to their respective agencies.

Then nothing happened. This impasse did not occur because of ill will, incompetence, or disagreement on fundamentals; rather, the inaction reflected the absence of top-down pressure for agencies to change their way of doing business. Mid-level officials in DOD and USAID might agree in principle with an idea, but they could not push it through their own bureaucracies without constant prodding from above.

EVENTUALLY, nearly a year later, the first Provincial Reconstruction Team (PRT) was fielded on the model I had suggested. USAID and State Department personnel were collocated with a military Civil Affairs team and housed within an American military base camp. The PRT concept has since been hailed as a major innovation in the field of post-conflict reconstruction. More than a dozen have been set up in Afghanistan (as in Iraq), with the United States running some and NATO allies overseeing others. These PRTs have developed into substantial organizations and have had some success pushing economic development into the countryside.

This arrangement nevertheless represents a second-best solution to the challenge of post-conflict reconstruction. When civilian officials need to live in military caserns, wear flack vests and helmets, and ride in military convoys, their capacity to enhance the overall reconstruction effort is significantly diminished. But deploying State and USAID officers to PRTs is certainly better than not sending them into the countryside at all. The preferable solution, back in 2002, would have been to deploy a multinational military presence with the stated mission of creating a secure environment in which civilian officials and normal citizens could circulate freely. It was done in Kabul with fewer than five thousand troops. It could have been done, at least for the other major population centers, with a considerably smaller force than was deployed several years later to repel a renewed Taliban insurgency.

The long delay in establishing the first PRTs was symptomatic of the lack of urgency with which the administration approached Afghan-related issues during these early months. The president and his top advisers had not forgotten about Afghanistan, but after the collapse of the Taliban and the installation of Hamid Karzai, that country had ceased to be their most pressing concern. Powell, Armitage, Rice, and Hadley would see me whenever I asked, but none of them ever asked to see me. This inattentiveness contrasted starkly with my experience under the previous administration. When I handled Haiti, Bosnia, or Kosovo, White House and State Department principals had bombarded me daily with questions, requests for status reports, or new instructions. This time around, weeks went by, and I heard nothing from my superiors.

The simple reason for this absence of proactive oversight was that my current bosses were not under presidential, congressional, public, or media pressure to produce early, visible results. Somalia, Haiti, Bosnia, and Kosovo had been tremendously controversial interventions. Large elements of Congress and the American public had been hostile to each enterprise. The press cast a constant and skeptical eye on the administration's performance. In 1994 the House reverted to Republican control, and in 1996 the Senate followed suit, after which Congress had become mercilessly inquisitive and consistently critical. This scrutiny kept the Clinton administration on its toes. Having led American troops into these alleged quagmires, the president needed to demonstrate that his reconstruction goals were being met and his exit strategies were on target. This pressure was conveyed downward from the White House to the involved cabinet officers and ultimately to me.

In 2002 President Bush was not under any pressure. He had just won the most popular war in American history. The military campaign in Afghanistan had gone unbelievably well, as had the diplomatic effort to install its successor government. His administration faced no demands to show results on Afghan reconstruction. Instead, the public was supportive, the press was laudatory, and Congress was docile. The president and his closest advisers felt they were at the top of their game. Insofar as Afghanistan was concerned, they believed that the hard part was over. They were moving on to other issues and planning the next campaign in the war on terror. Within weeks of the fall of

Kabul, those of us working on Afghanistan found ourselves in a backwater, operating within a larger bureaucracy that had other more pressing priorities.

IN APRIL I RECEIVED a call from a White House speechwriter. Bush was slated to speak at the Virginia Military Institute, where Stonewall Jackson had once taught and Gen. George C. Marshall had gone to school. "Would it be O.K.," the speechwriter asked, "if the president were to cite the Marshall Plan for post–World War II European reconstruction as the model for his efforts in Afghanistan?"

"Sure," I responded. If the president declared a Marshall Plan for Afghanistan, I thought, his administration would surely feel compelled to deliver on the promise. This assumption proved to be naive. The president did promise a Marshall Plan, but there was no follow-up to the speech whatsoever. No one at the State Department, the Office of Management and Budget (OMB), or the National Security Council initiated any effort to assess the requirements for a successful reconstruction effort. Not until the fall of 2002 did the administration ask Congress for additional money for Afghanistan. Most of that fund went to the Defense Department.

On taking the Afghan assignment, I had asked Deputy Secretary Armitage for authority over the allocation of reconstruction funding so that I could program what little there was to meet that country's most urgent needs. The director of USAID, Andrew Natsios, objected as soon as he heard of my request, not because he disagreed with my priorities—we never discussed them—but because he wanted to set his own. He insisted that aid to Afghanistan should be allocated in the same manner as for any other developing country, with his staff assessing the needs and with himself determining how the available money would be spent.

This situation turned into a classic Washington turf battle, all about status and prerogative. When Armitage proved unwilling to overrule Natsios, responsibility for overseeing Afghan reconstruction remained divided among half a dozen State Department and USAID fiefdoms: among these, two different offices handled humanitarian aid, another was responsible for police training, and USAID tackled economic development. Further, no one short of Armitage himself could shift resources from one category to the other as circumstances warranted. Armitage had many competing responsibilities and spent little time on these funding issues. Given the trifling amounts available, he had no real reason to do so.

At a practical level, my most immediate difference with Natsios came down to a choice between road building and agricultural assistance. Natsios wanted to spend USAID's limited funding to help farmers, many of whom would be returning refugees, to plant their next crop. Karzai's top priority, meanwhile, was to get American help in rebuilding the road from Kabul to Kandahar, thus linking his capital with the former Taliban stronghold and traditional center of Pashtun society.

USAID was certainly right that providing small farmers with seed and fertilizer would have a more immediate and substantial economic impact than hiring foreign contractors to begin a multiyear road-building project. It was also likely that the World Bank and other large donors would eventually come through with much larger sums than the United States could afford for that road. Karzai was equally correct, however, that early and visible work on the road linking Kabul to Kandahar would have the most immediate psychological impact on a population eager for signs that the war was over.

Had the decision rested with me, I would have split the infant aid program and addressed both priorities. In the end, we took this path, but only after months of debate, repeated appeals from Karzai, and a decision by President Bush to redirect the aid effort in his preferred direction. The time spent settling this relatively minor dispute signaled that the system for setting and implementing reconstruction policy was inadequate. Moreover, lacking the money to fund both priorities was evidence that the overall assistance levels were completely out of whack with the administration's rhetoric.

WHILE STILL IN KABUL, I had urged Rice to invite Karzai to Washington. I was confident, based on our brief acquaintance, that he would make a good impression on Congress and the media and get on well with President Bush. The White House accordingly issued an invitation, and in early February, Karzai made an official state visit. He let it be known that he would again press the case for ISAF expansion. The White House was eager to preempt further debate on that issue. Rather than rebuff Karzai completely, the Pentagon suggested that President Bush should take advantage of the visit and announce an American program to build a new Afghan national army. Since DOD had already agreed that the United States would take the lead in this sector, I saw no reason to oppose the announcement. I did not share, however, its proponents' view that this training program represented an alternative to deploying international peacekeepers. Optimists in the administration professed to believe that a new Afghan army might be created in six to twelve months. I knew from experience that six to twelve years was a more realistic figure.

As with the announcement of a Marshall Plan for Afghan reconstruction, I expected that this presidential initiative would generate an early and substantial effort to carry out the promise. Once again I was disappointed. The announcement instead set off a series of arguments about who should pay for the program and how extensive it should be.

The Defense Department, having pushed this initiative in order to deflect Karzai's interest in getting more peacekeeping troops, now insisted that the State Department pay for the Afghan army's training program. As absurd as this position might seem, there was precedent for this arrangement. In the mid-1990s, in the Balkans, DOD had managed to shift responsibility for military training to the State Department on the grounds that American troops should not undertake nation-building. Using former military personal for the actual instruction, the State Department had in fact done a creditable job of strengthening the Croatian and Bosnian armies. The American military, for its part, had then performed the peacekeeping mission. Now with regard to Afghanistan, DOD was refusing to do any peacekeeping, was discouraging anyone else from so doing, and was insisting that the State Department should pay for the military training program that DOD was touting as its solution to the Afghan security issue.

I rejected the proposal out of hand. My most persuasive argument was that the State Department did not have any money for this purpose. This point proved decisive.

After several weeks of interagency wrangling, DOD agreed to both manage and pay for the military training program. The Pentagon then sought to define the program's scope as narrowly as possible. It determined that American soldiers would train Afghan recruits, but the Afghan Ministry of Defense would be responsible for selecting the recruits, equipping and paying them, and supporting them once trained. Fahim Khan headed the Ministry of Defense and staffed it almost exclusively with Tajik officers loyal to him. The thought that Fahim's ministry would or could oversee the process of building a national army whose composition would reflect the country's ethnic makeup and geographic diversity was extremely naive.

I argued that the United States would have to get involved in selecting and training recruits for the new force. This point struck my DOD colleagues as a new idea, although it was standard practice in every other nation-building operation of which I was aware. They reluctantly agreed to run the issue up their chain of command. Of course, they meant to Secretary Rumsfeld, since no one else in that department was empowered to decide matters of such moment.

Several weeks later the answer came back down. The secretary had refused to countenance any American involvement in recruiting Afghan soldiers. An effort to promote ethnic and regional diversity of the new army would amount, Rumsfeld charged, to "social engineering," which the secretary apparently felt to be a bad thing.

This decision resulted in a year of almost entirely wasted effort. American soldiers trained the tens of thousands of recruits Fahim and the other warlords supplied, but nearly all of these deserted as soon as they finished their course of instruction. Fahim, like the other commanders, was perfectly satisfied with the army he had. He had no interest in building up a competitor and eventual replacement. He and other warlords thus offered up their least promising candidates for training. His ministry made little effort to support, pay, organize, or motivate the men who emerged from the American training program. Thus more than a year after kicking off the American effort, barely two thousand men remained under arms.

Eventually the U.S. military made a new start. Rumsfeld's ban on social engineering was reversed. Americans worked with the Afghan authorities to ensure the selection of a better-qualified, more ethnically and regionally diverse body of recruits while also assuming responsibility for helping organize, sustain, motivate, and lead the newly formed Afghan units once their training was complete. But a full year had been lost, and beyond the capital Afghanistan remained as insecure as ever.

WITHIN THE STATE Department I continued to wage a losing battle against bureaucratic inertia. Despite several months of effort, I had found neither people to man my operation nor a place to house them. I had asked for a staff of fifteen. Armitage had agreed, but only a couple of individuals had been hired. Afghanistan was apparently not the top priority for the State Department's personnel system. As for space, I was offered rooms in a building half a mile from the State Department, another indication of the importance attached to our work.

At this point we still had little reconstruction to oversee, so my lack of staff to do so was not particularly damaging. The State Department's slowness in gearing up for these responsibilities, however, reflected the lack of urgency that permeated the whole government's approach to Afghanistan.

The U.S. government had not always dragged its feet over nation-building. A few weeks after the liberation of Kosovo, in the fall of 1999, I was called into Secretary Albright's office, located one floor above my own. When Albright asked me whether I had enough staff to handle the new workload of reconstruction, I responded affirmatively, noting that I had three separate offices with a combined staff of about sixty working on Balkan issues.

"Not enough," Albright replied. "I want you to recruit additional people. Also, find two more ambassadorial-level deputies who can circulate in the region while you run things here in Washington. I want the Balkans awash with senior American envoys. I want everyone there to know that we care and that we are keeping an eye on them."

I soon discovered that the stimulus for this unusual if not unwelcome directive was a rumor that the White House was thinking of appointing its own Balkan envoy. Albright's move was designed to preempt any such power grab. Over the next few days I did indeed dispatch two additional roving envoys to join our already resident ambassadors in the region in overseeing reconstruction efforts and pressing Balkan leaders to live up to their commitments.

There was undoubtedly a degree of overkill in the number of American diplomats dispatched to Bosnia and Kosovo that year, as there was in the number of NATO troops deployed. In this case, the State Department had emulated DOD's embrace of the Powell doctrine of overwhelming force, which was based on a conviction that it is always easier to withdraw unnecessary assets than to reinforce a faltering enterprise.

Two years later I was overseeing a much more demanding effort in Afghanistan—a country five times larger than Bosnia and Kosovo combined and many times poorer—with a staff one-fifth the size. President Bush's top advisers were not vying with each other for control of this effort; instead, the White House had transferred oversight responsibility to the State Department. Rumsfeld was committed to the small-footprint, low-profile approach to nation-building. The State Department was going along with Rumsfeld, not because Powell thought this approach was sound but because he felt he had few resources to spare and knew the White House was not going to give him more.

PERHAPS THE SINGLE most frustrating experience of this period was my failure to secure an interagency agreement on how to compensate innocent Afghan victims of American firepower. One reason the Afghans had welcomed the American presence early on had been the almost unbelievable accuracy and carefully discriminated application of American firepower during the initial air campaign. While in Kabul Afghans had told me of how American missiles had taken out just the right vehicle in a line of cars or just the right room in a large building, killing Taliban or al Qaeda targets without harming the nearby civilians. True or not, these stories created high expectations that were slowly being dashed.

Perversely, the low number of American ground forces in Iraq probably boosted the number of civilian casualties. The minimalist approach Secretary Rumsfeld and General Franks favored required the substitution of firepower for manpower. In early 2002, only about eight thousand American troops were in country. Protecting the local population was not one of their tasks. The United States regarded its mission in Afghanistan as one of counterterrorism, not peacekeeping or even counterinsurgency; therefore, public security was not a mission objective. American forces did not target innocent civilians; indeed, they went to great lengths to avoid doing so inadvertently. But killing bad guys—not protecting good guys—was their mission, and airpower was often the chosen instrument.

All the Afghan people had had personal experiences with war, and they were prepared to put up with a certain level of collateral damage. When their friends—particularly their wealthy friends, the Americans—harmed them, they expected that their friends would take care of the unintended victims or their survivors somehow.

When I raised this issue and suggested that we look for some way to address the Afghans' expectation, my Defense Department colleagues responded with the ultimate bureaucratic stonewall. They told me, "This is a legal, not a policy issue, and as such, we cannot even discuss it. Your lawyers will need to talk to our lawyers."

Having been subjected to this treatment before, I knew it was a formula for deadlock. Lawyers are not necessarily obstructionist. Told to find a way forward, they will. Without such instructions, however, they will simply dig in and protect their client's position, impervious to logic or appeals to their better nature. In Rumsfeld's Pentagon, no one other than the secretary could release the DOD lawyers from this junkyard dog posture. So this issue remained unresolved for my tenure's duration.

The Pentagon's position was that we were still at war in Afghanistan. In wartime civilians have no right to compensation for any harm suffered as a byproduct of the conflict. I was prepared to concede that innocent victims might not have a right to such redress, provided that we agreed to afford them the privilege of it, especially since we needed their goodwill to win the war.

Like so many other early decisions regarding Afghan reconstruction, DOD eventually reversed its stance. In the summer of 2002 an American AC-130 gunship mistakenly strafed an Afghan wedding party, killing forty-eight innocent people and wounding over a hundred. Thereafter, DOD introduced a system of ex gratia payments to the victims or their survivors of such incidents. This practice has since become a standard procedure in both Afghanistan and Iraq. During those early months the United States had simply built up resentment and dissipated goodwill unnecessarily because no one in authority was willing to tell the lawyers to construct an acceptable rationale for such payments.

My inability to broker an agreement for compensating innocent Afghan victims of American firepower illustrates the difficulty of trying to run an interagency process from one of the departments involved. DOD eventually came to the conclusion that such payments were necessary after commanders in the field pressured them. Prodding from the State Department, by contrast, simply put the Defense Department on the defensive.

THE BUSH ADMINISTRATION might have been turning its attention toward the next campaign in its global war on terror, but the international community remained focused on Afghanistan. In March in Geneva, I organized a second series of meetings among those who might contribute to rebuilding the Afghan security sector. First I met with a core group of major powers, including representatives of the British, French, German, Italian, Japanese, Russian, and Canadian governments. At this meeting we confirmed the lead nation commitments discussed earlier in Tokyo and updated each other on the limited progress made in fulfilling them. On the second day I held a larger meeting at which several dozen governments were represented, including all the major regional powers. We gathered at the United Nations Office in Geneva, Switzerland. As had been the case in Tokyo, both Brahimi and Foreign Minister Abdullah joined me.

In this larger gathering Pakistan and India again expressed a keen interest in supporting the development of the Afghan army. My old friend Ambassador Lambha introduced me to an Indian Army general who spoke at length about how his government could build a professional Afghan military. I listened politely but made no promises. Again, given the intense antipathy between India and Pakistan, which were then still on the brink of war, their joint collaboration on any project, let alone one this sensitive to both, struck me as improbable.

Iran was also represented by several diplomats who had been with us in Bonn, including Ambassador Taherian, now Tehran's envoy in Kabul. The Iranians asked to meet with me separately after the larger session. We gathered in the coffee shop of the InterContinental Hotel. They too had in tow a general in full uniform. He had commanded the Iranian assistance mission to the Northern Alliance throughout the recent civil war.

"My government is prepared to participate in an American-led program of support to the new Afghan army," the general said. "Specifically, Iran is prepared to build barracks for and train up to twenty thousand troops in a larger effort under your leadership."

"If Iran trains some Afghan troops and the United States trains others," I responded warily, "might not the two groups end up with incompatible doctrines?"

"Don't worry," the general replied, smiling, "we are still using the manuals you left behind in 1979."

"Well, all right," I conceded, "so maybe they would have compatible doctrines. But they might develop conflicting loyalties."

"Iran has trained, equipped, and, by the way, is still paying the Afghan troops your military is now using to hunt down remaining Taliban elements," he pointed out. "Are you having any difficulty with their loyalty?"

"No," I admitted, "not that I know of." I promised to report their offer to Washington.

This unexpected offer struck me as problematic in detail but promising in its overall implications. Despite the general's assurances, I could foresee problems in having Iran and the United States training different components of a new Afghan army. But the Iranians' participation, under American leadership, in a joint program of this sort would be a breathtaking advance after more than twenty years of mutual hostility. This offer also represented a significant step beyond the quiet diplomatic cooperation we had achieved so far. Clearly, despite having been relegated to the "axis of evil," the Khatami government still wanted to deepen its cooperation with Washington and was prepared to do so in an overt and public fashion.

Back home, I immediately went to see Powell.

"Very interesting," he responded to my account of this conversation. "You need to talk to Condi."

So I went to see Rice.

"Interesting," she said. "You need to talk to Don."

Several days later Rice arranged a meeting of NSC principals to discuss the Iranian offer, among other matters. When we came to that item on the agenda, I again recounted my conversation with the Iranians. Rumsfeld did not look up from the papers he was perusing. When I finished, he made no comment and asked no questions. Neither did anyone else. After a long pause, seeing no one ready to take up the issue, Rice moved the meeting on to the next item on her agenda. The Iranians never received a response.

10

AFTERWARD

ON THE LAST DAY IN APRIL, Colin Powell marked my retirement with generous remarks, an outsized medal, and an affectionate hug before an audience of friends, colleagues, and family.

I left government service still frustrated with the pace of Afghan reconstruction and puzzled by the administration's seeming neglect, but in no sense was I bitter or regretful. For more than thirty years I had enjoyed a succession of fascinating jobs. I was particularly grateful that Powell gave me a final opportunity to serve my country after the 9/11 attacks and that other old friends, like Condoleezza Rice, Steve Hadley, and George Tenet, had supported me throughout my most recent mission. I discounted the talk already circulating in Washington about an invasion of Iraq. I felt the administration would come to see, soon enough, the real needs in Afghanistan.

The next day I showed up at my new workplace, the RAND Corporation, a think tank known for its work on national security issues. After a lifetime in government service, I was anxious to avoid the letdown that might come from even a brief period of inactivity. The strategy worked. Soon I was turning my nation-building experience into grist for a new career, producing a series of RAND studies on the subject.

Colin Powell contacted me a couple of times in the succeeding months to see whether I wanted to return. The Afghan reconstruction effort had flagged, and President Bush was becoming increasingly impatient. USAID, the State Department, and DOD were blaming each other for the lack of progress. The civilians argued development could not happen without security, but the military countered there could be no security without economic growth. No one faced up to Afghanistan's basic problem, its overall lack of resources. Total international assistance for Afghanistan was still running at fifty dollars per Afghan annually. No international peacekeepers worked outside Kabul. Thus while the capital was secure and increasingly prosperous, the countryside was still unsafe and economically stagnant.

Philip Zelikow, a confidant of Rice's and a former colleague from the Bush administration, asked me to look over an early draft of what would become the National Security Strategy report of 2002. Somewhat later he also requested that I write a policy paper on Iraq for Rice. Neither contribution had any apparent impact. The National Security Strategy, when it appeared, endorsed the concept of preemption to deal with not just imminent threats but grave and growing ones. Saddam Hussein's alleged possession of weapons of mass destruction, contrary to my advice, remained the report's lead justification for invading Iraq.

ZALMAY KHALILZAD still worked in the National Security Council. Like many others in the administration's upper reaches, his main preoccupation had become Iraq. Early in 2003 he invited me to his office in the Old Executive Office Building, adjoining the White House, to discuss the formation of a new Iraqi government. The invasion was only weeks away, yet the administration was still debating what to install in Saddam's place. The leading possibility was an extended American occupation, which would likely be unpopular in the region, and perhaps in Iraq. Planners were considering, therefore, the Afghan alternative—that is, the rapid formation of a successor regime that could be put in place within weeks of Saddam's removal. Khalilzad wanted my opinion: did I think this plan might be feasible?

I said that it was worth trying, but it would likely prove more difficult than had been our experience with Afghanistan. Several obstacles to replicating the Afghan model existed. First, Iraq did not have an indigenous resistance movement akin to the Northern Alliance upon which a new regime could be based. All known opponents to Saddam were dead or in exile. Many had been out of the country for years, with some of the most prominent absent for decades. Few of these potential leaders enjoyed any significant support inside Iraq. Those who did were based in Iran, making them unattractive choices.

A year earlier at the Petersberg, Khalilzad and I needed only to persuade the Northern Alliance leaders, who by then effectively controlled much of Afghanistan, to accept an admixture of émigrés in order to produce a broadly based government that could immediately achieve local acceptance and international recognition. Iraq did not have such a group upon which to build a new government.

Further, Iraq's neighboring states were also likely to be much less helpful this time around. Not only was the American rationale for invading Iraq weak, but nearly all the regional states would also likely oppose the American vision for Hussein's successor. Again, the U.S. position was different from what Khalilzad and I had to work with a year earlier. The United States had not gone into Afghanistan promising to make that country a democratic model for Central Asia, with the intention of thereby undermining the legitimacy of all neighboring regimes in order to see them eventually replaced by democratic governments. Had America declared this purpose, Washington would not have gotten bases in Tajikistan and Uzbekistan, overflight rights from Pakistan, or help from Russia and Iran in reconciling the various Afghan factions and installing the Karzai regime.

With Iraq, by contrast, the Bush administration was already asserting its intention of making Iraq a model democracy as a first step toward promoting similar changes throughout the region. The governments of Saudi Arabia, Syria, Jordan, or Iran were not likely to embrace this project. Even Turkey, a democracy and a NATO ally, would be deeply hostile to the idea because of the boost it would likely give to Kurdish nationalism. American efforts to bring the Iraqi factions together into a broadly based national government were, therefore, unlikely to receive the kind of support from neighboring governments that Khalilzad and I had been able to muster in Bonn.

Khalilzad also acknowledged that the administration would not accept a UN role comparable to that which Brahimi had played in Bonn. Washington was extremely unhappy over the UN Security Council's refusal to endorse the forthcoming invasion. Likewise, the United Nations was not much happier with Washington. Without the world body's sponsorship and endorsement, getting both Iraqi and international acceptance of any government that might emerge from an American-led selection process would be more difficult. Nevertheless, given the problems associated with a prolonged American occupation, the option of trying to form an Iraqi successor regime seemed worth trying.

Khalilzad and I also discussed U.S. relations with Iran. On my departure from the State Department, he had inherited responsibility for conducting what remained of that dialogue. In a few days he was scheduled to hold another session with Javad Zarif, who had moved from the Iranian Foreign Ministry to head Tehran's Mission to the United Nations, but was still Tehran's designated interlocutor with the United States. Despite the fact that Zarif now lived in New York, the administration neither allowed Zarif to attend meetings in Washington nor permitted Khalilzad to go to New York for that purpose. Instead, their infrequent gatherings still took place in Geneva, out of sight of both the American and Iranian media.

As I was leaving, Khalilzad asked whether I would call Zarif to clarify one minor administrative detail related to their upcoming meeting. If he sent his inquiry through regular channels—that is, through the American Embassy in Bern to the Swiss Embassy in Tehran to the Iranian Foreign Ministry to reach Zarif in New York—Zarif's answer, which would have to follow the same track in reverse, was unlikely to arrive in time. Shaking my head in despair at the obstacles both American and Iranian policy erected to even the simplest communication, I promised to call Zarif. Later I relayed Khalilzad's message and passed back Zarif's answer.

That winter's meeting between Zarif and Khalilzad turned out to be the last U.S.-Iranian exchange for some time. Shortly thereafter the Bush administration cut off further contact. At issue was an American request for access to suspected al Qaeda operatives being held in Tehran. The Iranians agreed but asked in return for similar access to the leaders of an anti-Iranian terrorist group held in U.S. custody in Iraq. Washington refused and cut off further exchanges. A few months later, despite this rebuff, the Iranian Foreign Ministry sent to the State Department via the Swiss ambassador in Tehran a paper outlining proposed solutions to the full range of issues dividing the two countries. Washington never considered the proposals and once again did not respond to the Iranians.

The Khatami government had twice made substantial cooperative overtures to Washington, the first after the Americans' victory in Afghanistan and the second after the U.S. invasion of Iraq. In both cases, the United States had eliminated grave threats to Iran's security. Now American troops were positioned on Iran's borders. These actions gave Tehran powerful incentives, both positive and negative, to mend relations with Washington. But while the Khatami regime felt both vulnerable and grateful, the Bush administration thought itself invincible. Why settle with Iran's revolutionary government when an opportunity to replace it might be just around the corner? Mullah Omar and Saddam Hussein had been overthrown in little more than a year. Might not the regime in Tehran follow in due course?

A FEW DAYS after my meeting with Khalilzad I was afforded another look at the administration's planning for post-Hussein Iraq. Since leaving the government, I had been invited from time to time to "opinion-leader" briefings Rumsfeld's Public Affairs staff had organized. The Pentagon took these occasions to inform and influence experts who wrote or spoke on defense-related issues. The meetings generally involved a dozen or so academics, retired generals, and representatives from various Washington policy institutes. Routinely, mid-level DOD officials briefed the listeners for an hour or two on topical issues, followed by a shorter session with the secretary himself. These meetings were not true exchanges. The Defense Department did not ask us for advice. The secretary and his staff did make themselves available for questioning, however, which was more than anyone at the State Department or the White House was doing, so we were grateful.

On one occasion Bill Luti conducted one of the initial briefings. Since our time together, he had moved up a notch and become a key Rumsfeld adviser on Iraq. His presentation was a typical Pentagon product, conveyed with the assistance of PowerPoint slides projected on a large screen. It covered planning for the American occupation. Joining Luti for the briefing was Jay Garner, a retired lieutenant general who had just been appointed head of the Office of Reconstruction and Humanitarian Assistance (ORHA) for Iraq. Luti explained that Garner and his team would deploy to Iraq with American and coalition forces, assume responsibility for meeting the population's immediate humanitarian needs, and oversee what was left of the Iraqi government. Sometime thereafter, Luti stated, a more senior American official, perhaps a former governor or ambassador, would succeed Garner and administer Iraq until a new constitution could be written, elections held, and a democratic Iraqi government installed. Garner also acknowledged that he expected to be replaced after a while by someone more senior.

A couple of other presentations followed Luti's. Then Rumsfeld joined us. As usual, he made no opening statement but just invited questions, which mostly related to the upcoming war. One attendee asked how long the American occupation of Iraq might last.

"I think the approach we took in Afghanistan offers a good model," Rumsfeld replied. "We should work with Iraqi opposition leaders to identify and put in place a new government that can quickly take office once Saddam is toppled."

Clearly two post-invasion alternatives for Iraq were still being considered within the Bush administration and even inside the Pentagon. One, which Luti outlined, was the Douglas MacArthur model, a conscious effort to imitate the successful post–World War II efforts to rebuild Germany and Japan. The alternative, or Karzai model, apparently still had its supporters, including the secretary of defense.

In the end, the MacArthur model prevailed, but only after Khalilzad and Garner had spent several weeks following the fall of Baghdad trying to identify locally credible leaders who were untainted by association with Saddam Hussein and who might make up a new government. Eventually, as Iraq descended into chaos, Washington lost patience with these efforts and reverted to its original plan, installing Ambassador L. Paul Bremer at the head of an American-run occupation regime. Bremer, in turn, insisted that the United States only needed one envoy in Iraq, and Khalilzad's mission was brought to an end.

Bremer had been Henry Kissinger's chief of staff at the State Department during the Nixon and Ford administrations. He had held several other posts, including ambassador to the Netherlands and head of the State

Department's Counterterrorism Office, before rejoining Kissinger in private practice. Bremer left government service in the late 1980s, just before the post–Cold War surge in nation-building. Had Bremer remained in the Foreign Service, he probably would have become involved in one or more of those interventions, as he had the quick wits and commanding presence such circumstances demand.

Bremer asked to see me shortly after his appointment to the Coalition Provisional Authority (CPA). He was anxious for any advice I could give him regarding his new responsibilities. By chance, I had just finished a study of seven American-led nation-building operations conducted over the past sixty years, and in its conclusion I suggested how the lessons gleaned from those operations might be applied in Iraq. I was able to give Bremer the galley proofs of this book, *America's Role in Nation-Building: From Germany to Iraq*, which RAND published in 2003.

This study made several points relevant to the situation Bremer would face. First, our research had found an inverse correlation between the number of occupying troops and the level of casualties suffered. In other words, the larger the occupying force, the less resistance it encountered. This deduction was inconsistent with Secretary Rumsfeld's preference for minimal deployments.

The RAND study also noted that one occupying soldier for every fifty inhabitants had often proved necessary to pacify and secure societies with serious internal divisions like Bosnia, Kosovo, or, potentially, Iraq. For Bosnia this arithmetic had produced a stabilization force of 60,000 personnel; for Kosovo, 50,000. For Iraq the number this analysis generated was 500,000. While the Clinton administration had adhered to these guidelines, the Bush administration, I warned Bremer, had no intention of doing so. On the contrary, even as we spoke the Pentagon was withdrawing American troops from Iraq. It intended bringing down U.S. force levels there to around 70,000 soldiers by the fall, I warned, in the hope that the number could be further reduced to about 40,000 by year's end.

"You are going to be sent out there with insufficient backing and then left to take the blame when things fall apart," I said.

As he relates in his own memoir, Bremer immediately brought the RAND study to the attention of both Rumsfeld and the president in an effort to boost the declining troop presence. He sent the secretary a copy of its summary chapter. Bremer's effort was successful to a point. Faced with mounting violence throughout the country, the Pentagon reversed its policy and started deploying more people to Iraq. Within a few months of Bremer's arrival in Baghdad, the number of U.S. and allied soldiers mounted to about 160,000 personnel. There the number stalled for the next several years.

The troop numbers in the RAND study were by no means out of line with other estimates. Tommy Franks's immediate predecessor as CENTCOM commander, Marine Gen. Anthony Zinni, had planned to occupy Iraq with 450,000 troops. Gen. Eric Shinseki, the Army chief of staff, testified to Congress a few weeks before the war began that it would take "several hundred thousand troops" to stabilize Iraq. Condi Rice's own staff, using the same comparative arithmetic as the RAND study, produced a paper for her that cited similar numbers.

Some weeks later a friend in the Pentagon told me that a request had come down from above for a memo explaining why the RAND analysis on troop numbers was wrong. I could easily understand why our conclusions were unwelcome. If one really needed 500,000 thousand troops to secure Iraq, then the United States probably should not have tried it in the first place. The American military establishment was not large enough to generate such force levels for any length of time.

Shortly after his arrival in Baghdad, Bremer telephoned to ask for help in staffing his mission. The Defense Department, which was responsible for manning the CPA, had proved unable to supply the numbers or types of individuals needed to govern Iraq. The State Department had sent Bremer a handful of good officers, but it did not extend itself greatly to find more. I gave him a list of individuals with whom I had served in Haiti and the Balkans, several of whom he was able to recruit. I also arranged to lend him half a dozen RAND staffers to fill key positions within the CPA.

MY WORK KEPT me abreast of general developments in Iraq and Afghanistan. As the situation in both countries continued to deteriorate, the administration became more open to advice, although it usually solicited information too late and seldom on the essentials. In 2004 as part of an effort to shift DOD's policy management of the occupation back to the White House, Rice recalled Robert Blackwill from New Delhi so that he could oversee operations in both Afghanistan and Iraq. Blackwill asked RAND for advice both on the upcoming transfer of sovereignty to an interim Iraqi government and on the coincident shift from DOD to the State Department for responsibility for the diplomatic and civil aspects of the American efforts there.

Within the administration, Blackwill was arguing in favor of having the United Nations oversee the selection of the new Iraq government, as it had done with Afghanistan in late 2001. I suggested Brahimi would be ideal for this role and arranged a dinner meeting for them at my home. Shortly thereafter they both headed off to Baghdad, where, along with Bremer, they put together Iraq's first post-Hussein government.

I urged Blackwill to create a regional forum through which the United States could engage Iraq's neighbors in a continuous and structured fashion about that country's future. My own experience in the Balkans and Afghanistan convinced me that the behavior of neighboring states could make or break any nation-building enterprise. Blackwill liked the idea. So did Brahimi, who was then installed in New York as UN secretary general Kofi Annan's top man for the Middle East. Unfortunately, Blackwill could never convince the rest of the administration to pursue the idea, and Brahimi could not proceed to create this group without the Americans' agreement.

John Negroponte was named the U.S. ambassador to Iraq and replaced Bremer as the Coalition Provisional Authority gave way to an American Embassy. Among the recommendations I had given Blackwill was shifting Iraq's assistance away from the massive construction projects the CPA initiated to programs that would rebuild the Iraqi security forces and improve the new government's capacity to deliver essential public services. Negroponte liked this approach and asked whether I would accompany him and head the reconstruction effort. Just as I had when Bremer made a similar request, I declined, but I did recommend another officer with recent and relevant experience in Afghanistan whom Negroponte hired and who instituted the suggested changes.

TO HIS CREDIT, Secretary Rumsfeld continued to bring selected analysts and commentators, including critics like myself, into the Pentagon once or twice a year for his opinion-leader briefings. Another revealing moment came in late 2004, when two colonels briefed such a group on the growth of Iraqi security forces. Rebuilding these forces had managed to be both tardy and rushed, as the process began late and then was hurried to make up for lost time. One colonel flashed a slide on the screen indicating that the Iraqi army and police forces had reached a combined total of 110,000 men.

The second colonel interrupted. "That number should be 125,000," he corrected.

"No. I checked it last night. It's 110,000," the first colonel insisted.

"We added 15,000 this morning," the second explained.

This was policy by PowerPoint at its worst. Clearly the numbers on the charts bore no relationship to the actual capacity of Iraqi security forces, which could hardly have gone up by 10 percent overnight. Yet these figures were not generated just for public consumption. They represented the actual basis on which the administration made important policy decisions.

An hour or so later, Rumsfeld arrived to answer questions. Michael O'Hanlon of the Brookings Institution pressed him for a figure on civilian casualties. As was his wont with unwelcome questions, Rumsfeld dismissed the subject airily. Baghdad's homicide rate was no more relevant to Iraq's stability, Rumsfeld insisted, than Detroit's homicide rate was to that of the United States.

Rumsfeld was not trying to avoid an unwelcome question. Even had he wanted to, the secretary of defense could not have provided a reliable number for Iraqi civilian casualties. No one in the U.S. occupation force had been instructed to collect these figures, and no one in Washington was charged with keeping count. Indeed, they had been told *not* to do so. Thus Rumsfeld did not simply claim that the number of Iraqi civilian deaths was irrelevant; he genuinely believed it. For all intensive purposes, so did the rest of the U.S. government.

In late 2005, at yet another of these opinion-leader briefings, I pressed Secretary Rumsfeld again on the issue of civilian casualty levels. By then, President Bush had estimated, in response to a journalist's question, that perhaps twenty thousand innocent Iraqis had been killed.

"Almost every week Iraq is losing a proportion of its population equal to the loss suffered by the United States on 9/11," I noted, citing President Bush's estimate. "Imagine, if you will, the impact on the American psyche if the United States was suffering a 9/11-scale attack every week, month after month."

In his response, the secretary denied that a civil war was under way. As evidence he pointed to the absence of any large numbers of refugees.

THROUGH 2006 I joined numerous other experts in advising the Iraq Study Group (ISG). My old boss James Baker and former congressman Lee Hamilton cochaired this congressionally mandated commission, which comprised a dozen prominent former officials known for their pragmatism, moderation, and wisdom. They in turn assembled experts who were more familiar than they with Iraq, its region, and the techniques of counterinsurgency, counterterrorism, and nation-building.

My main contribution to this effort was to argue in favor of what became known as the "diplomatic surge," or the initiation of an intensified regional diplomatic campaign designed to engage all Iraq's neighbors in a last-ditch effort to hold that country together. I noted that the Bosnian civil war could not have been stopped without involving the two countries responsible for it, Serbia and Croatia, and the two men personally responsible for the resultant genocide, President Milosevic and President Franjo Tudjman. Both these men had been invited to the peace conference in Dayton, and both had become privileged U.S. partners in implementing that accord. We could easily have adduced moral arguments against elevating them in that fashion, but if we had allowed those considerations to govern American policy, the war in Bosnia would still be raging.

I also cited the constructive role that all Afghanistan's neighboring states had played at the Bonn Conference as evidence of the important dividends such regional diplomacy could pay. I argued that only a comparable effort could stave off an intensified civil war in Iraq. The Iraqi Study Group was convinced and made this diplomatic push one of the two main themes of its report.

The group's work proceeded slowly. Baker felt, reasonably enough, that any recommendations released before the November 2006 mid-term elections would be quickly dismissed in the heat of the political campaign. Several other members, including former defense secretary Bill Perry and former Supreme Court justice Sandra Day O'Connor, were impatient with the delay. They feared the situation in Iraq might deteriorate beyond repair by the time the group made its recommendations.

In any event, delaying the report until after the mid-term elections still did not secure it a positive reception in the White House. The ISG presented its recommendations to President Bush in December 2006. In January 2007 the president brushed aside this bipartisan effort and chose instead to intensify the U.S. confrontation with Iran.

11

THE RETURN OF THE TALIBAN

THE AFGHAN CAMPAIGN OF 2001 provides a textbook illustration of the successful integration of force and diplomacy and of the benefit derived from linking national power to international legitimacy.

In the weeks after 9/11 every agency of the American government worked toward a common goal with minimal friction. In the Afghan campaign, the CIA ran paramilitary operations, DOD ran the military, and the State Department oversaw the diplomacy. Each deferred to the other in its sphere of competence. This unhesitating collaboration was of immense assistance to me while spearheading the diplomatic effort. The CIA put together the overall strategy for the war and guided the application of American military power in support of a local insurgency. The agency also kept me in contact with the key Afghan actors, either delivering me to them or them to me. The devastating effect of U.S. precision bombing gave decisive weight to American diplomacy. The secretary of state gave me the authority and latitude to broker an agreement on the makeup of a successor regime. White House support for my effort was unwavering, and every element of American power and influence was brought to bear. Better yet, by operating with broad international support, the weight of the entire international system also backed my efforts.

Unfortunately, this harmony proved short lived. By late December 2001 the American military presence in Afghanistan had grown from a few hundred men to several thousand soldiers. As a result, the locus of decision making increasingly moved from the CIA and the State Department to the Defense

Department. The Pentagon leadership determined that American soldiers would not do peacekeeping, their usual post-combat role. On the other hand, the Pentagon had U.S. troops dispense humanitarian and reconstruction assistance, provide Hamid Karzai's personal security, and build a new Afghan army, all functions that had been State Department responsibilities in previous nation-building missions. Thus, DOD had the money, DOD had the dominant presence on the ground, and the DOD leadership had its own clear idea about how the post-combat phase should be handled.

When Washington's attention turned to Iraq, the synergy achieved by fully harnessing CIA, DOD, and State Department capabilities eroded further. In Iraq, the secretary of defense directed all civil as well as military functions. Even the brilliant use of the CIA's paramilitary capabilities in Afghanistan did not serve as a model. Secretary of Defense Rumsfeld had been discomfited by DOD's dependence on the CIA for these capabilities. After the victorious Afghan campaign, his department began to build a competing and redundant capacity.

An even greater loss of synergy took place at the international level. The speedy and thorough American victory in Afghanistan demonstrated how much could be achieved when all elements of the U.S. government operated in harmony with the international community and particularly with the regional powers most likely to have influence on the country in question. But neither the administration, nor, truth be told, Congress or the American people drew this lesson. Few Americans recognized how much the United States owed to the improbable coalition that had helped it topple the Taliban and install a moderate, cooperative successor regime in its place. Rather, America's rapid victory in 2001 left the dominant impression of near omnipotence.

This overconfidence resulted in an Iraqi campaign that overlooked nearly all the advantages of interagency and international collaboration that had delivered success in Afghanistan. The conventional military victory was still impressive, but the political and economic follow-thorough ran into immediate and rapidly mounting difficulties. If the Afghan campaign showed how much the United States could achieve with interagency collaboration and international support, the U.S. effort in Iraq has illustrated how little can be accomplished without them.

The United States was able to garner and retain other countries' support for its intervention in Afghanistan because Washington espoused objectives for that campaign that the rest of the world and, in particular, the neighboring states could embrace—namely, an end to terror and civil war. Little more than a year later the Bush administration wrapped its next intervention in rhetoric that the international community and, again, in particular, the neighboring governments were certain to reject—that is, preemption and democratization.

While the Bonn Conference was still under way Secretary Rumsfeld had instructed General Franks to begin planning another invasion. Throughout the next sixteen months the dominant issue in Washington was not how to rebuild Afghanistan but how to overrun Iraq. Strengthening Karzai took second place to overthrowing Saddam Hussein. Once this goal had been achieved, rebuilding Iraq then continued to overshadow Afghan reconstruction.

Each of these two nation-building operations proved perversely unhelpful to the other. The deceptive ease with which a moderate, broadly popular, and highly cooperative successor was installed to replace the Taliban strongly influenced the planning for Iraq. If the notoriously isolated and xenophobic Afghans welcomed their liberators, would not the more urbane and secular Iraqis do the same? If a few thousand American troops were sufficient to bring Afghanistan's long-running civil war to an end, would it not be even easier to prevent such a con-flict in Iraq? If Afghanistan could be rebuilt for an average cost of fifty dollars per Afghan annually, could not the much richer and much less-damaged Iraq pay for its own reconstruction? And finally, if the talented and experienced men and women at the top echelons of the Bush administration could polish off the Taliban in a matter of weeks, should not this same crack national security team be able to guide American policy to an equally easy and quick success in Iraq? These questions all seemed to have easy, obvious answers.

It is instructive, in this regard, to compare the longer-term effects of the Clinton and Bush administrations' first experiences in employing armed force. Preoccupied by other matters during its early months in office, Clinton's national security team steadily reduced the number of American troops in Somalia while simultaneously expanding the mission of the residual U.S. combat force there. What had begun as an American-led effort to deliver food and medicine to famine victims became a UN-directed program to deliver grassroots democracy. Somali warlords had been willing enough to accommodate the delivery of relief supplies, some of which they could divert to their own purposes, but they were much less inclined to tolerate a democratization campaign designed to displace them. Rather quickly this mismatch between plummeting capabilities and soaring ambitions caught up with the residual U.S. force. It resulted in the firefight in downtown Mogadishu that caused eighteen American combat deaths. The effect on the Clinton administration was profoundly chastening. The president replaced both his secretary of defense and White House chief of staff. Other members of Bill Clinton's national security team knew that their own jobs and reputations hung by a thread. They recognized that they could lose both in the event of another slip. One year into the Clinton administration, no one, least of all the president and his top advisers, held an exaggerated sense of their capacity to wisely wield military power.

President Clinton did go on to invade three more countries. In each subsequent case, however, his administration exercised a degree of forward planning, worst-case risk assessment, and prudent hedging against unforeseen eventualities that was largely missing from his successor's preparations for the occupation of Iraq. Never again did Clinton's civilian advisers ignore military counsel or deny commanders in the field the reinforcements they felt necessary to do their job. Colin Powell was gone, but his doctrine of overwhelming force lived on. Each of the Clinton administration's subsequent interventions were super-sized, with commanders deploying military forces so overwhelming in numbers and combat power they discouraged the very thought of violent resistance.

If the Somalia debacle instilled a sense of caution in the Clinton team, as well as in the national psyche, that sometimes seemed nearly paralyzing, the Afghan triumph promoted a sense of self-confidence that verged on the reckless. Hubris affected not just the Bush administration. Congress, the press, and the American public were also swept up in the same mood. While 9/11 made the invasion of Iraq seem justified, the Afghan campaign made it seem feasible. In 1991 President George H. W. Bush had been lucky to get a bare majority of Congress to vote for liberating Kuwait, despite a transparently compelling justification for war. In 2002, his son received an overwhelming congressional mandate to invade Iraq, despite a much weaker casus belli.

Before Hamid Karzai had even taken office, stabilizing Afghanistan had ceased to be the Bush administration's top foreign policy priority. Throughout 2002, while al Qaeda and the Taliban licked their wounds across the border in Pakistan, no serious effort was made to extend Kabul's authority to the provinces that had been the traditional Taliban strongholds. This neglect continued through most of 2003, as manpower, money, and the psychic energy of America's leaders flowed into Iraq. Not until 2004 did American assistance to Afghanistan begin to rise sharply. Only in 2005 were significant numbers of international peacekeepers deployed outside Kabul and only in 2006 were they deployed in any number in the south, where a Taliban resurgence was already under way.

Nevertheless, it would be unfair to attribute the Bush administration's failure to resource its Afghan expedition solely to its focus on Iraq. After all, Iraq was undoubtedly the administration's top priority, yet that operation was also under-resourced in its initial stages. The administration probably would have undermanned and underfunded the Afghan reconstruction even if its attention had not shifted to Iraq so early. The simple fact is that the Bush administration had entered office determined not to continue its predecessor's nation-building efforts. Whatever Clinton did, Bush was going to do differently and, in particular, more economically.

In contrast to Iraq, where the situation began to deteriorate rapidly after the fall of Baghdad, the picture in Afghanistan has been more mixed. Security has slowly worsened, but both politically and economically, the country has continued to move ahead.

Rather remarkably, all the benchmarks laid out in the Bonn Agreement were met more or less on schedule. In mid-2002 a loya jirga convened. Afghan leaders from all over the country met, endorsed the results of the Bonn Conference, and chose Hamid Karzai as the country's interim president. A second loya jirga, held in January 2004, adopted a new constitution, one of the most progressive in the Muslim world. Presidential elections were held in October of that year. Balloting was peaceful, and participation rates were high. Karzai was elected with more than 55 percent of the vote, defeating twenty-two other candidates. In 2005 legislative elections were held. Again, balloting was generally peaceful and participation high.

Much of the credit for this progress must go to Lakhdar Brahimi, who headed the UN mission in Kabul until 2004. Also instrumental was Zalmay Khalilzad, who took charge of the American Embassy in late 2003 and remained for nearly two years. Both men were able to exercise great influence because of their long-established personal relationships with various Afghan leaders, their presence "at the creation" in Bonn, and their close ties with their respective bosses, the UN secretary general in Brahimi's case and with the president of the United States in Khalilzad's. None of their successors have brought quite the same authority to the job.

While consolidating his government Karzai gradually shed his dependence on the three men most responsible for his original elevation: Younis Qanooni, Mohammed Fahim, and Abdullah Abdullah. Qanooni was the first to go. Demoted in 2003 from interior to education minister, he left the government in 2004 to run against Karzai in the presidential election and emerged as the runner-up. In 2005 he was elected to the Parliament and then to the chairmanship of its lower house, in which capacity he has effectively emerged as a leader of the opposition to the Karzai government. He has exercised this function in a generally responsible manner.

Fahim was disappointed when he was not chosen as Karzai's running mate in the 2005 presidential election. Afterward, he was replaced as the defense minister. Abdullah stayed on as foreign minister until 2006, when he too was replaced.

These three protégés of Ahmed Shah Massoud were bound to lose their grip on the principal levers of power eventually. The faction they represented was simply too small to sustain a claim on the three most important cabinet-level posts. Tajiks constitute perhaps a fifth of the Afghan population, and those from the strategically located Panjshir Valley, from which Massoud's forces had threatened the capital throughout twenty years of civil war, were no more than a fraction of that. The Pakistani government was also strongly opposed to all three men, a sentiment that the trio largely reciprocated. Pashtun leaders pressed Karzai to broaden his government's base by providing them more posts, particularly the most powerful ones.

Economically, Afghanistan has also progressed, albeit a good deal more slowly than hoped. By 2007, the country's per capita income had doubled, yet it remains among the poorest countries in the world. A portion of its growth has come from burgeoning drug production, which lifts the incomes of some but funds both government corruption and antigovernment resistance.

While political and economic trends have, on balance, been positive, the security situation has gradually worsened. Year after year the number of terrorist attacks has increased, having tripled from 2002 to 2007.

After a false start and wasted year, American-led training of a new Afghan army slowly began to produce reasonably capable units. German and then American support for the police, however, proved woefully inadequate. Modest British efforts to stem illegal drug production were overwhelmed by the scale of the problem. Italian support for judicial reform was even more modest in scope and accomplishment. A Japanese-funded disarmament program did have some success. The larger armies that generals like Fahim, Dostum, and Ismail Khan commanded have largely been disbanded, but much of the country remains under the control of smaller, less heavily armed militias.

The renewed civil war in Afghanistan can be attributed to two fundamental causes. The United States, the Karzai administration, and the rest of the international community failed to take advantage of the lull that followed the Taliban regime's collapse in late 2001 to project government services, including security, out into the countryside. The second cause was that the regional consensus in support of the Karzai government reached at the Petersberg had eroded. In the aftermath of that collective achievement, the United States and the rest of the international community had a golden occasion to help Afghans build a government capable of providing its population with at least basic public services. Al Qaeda was smashed, with its remaining members forced into hiding, and the Taliban was discredited and dispersed. Neither was capable of posing an immediate threat to the new regime in Kabul. The Bush administration, however, failed to seize that opportunity.

Throughout 2002 and 2003 U.S. and international assistance was minimal. While blame for that negligence must be widely shared, the failure principally reflected the American administration's early aversion to nation-building.

Well into 2003 the administration touted the merits of its low-profile, small-footprint alternative. In speeches and newspaper articles Donald Rumsfeld maintained that generous international assistance to Bosnia and Kosovo had turned those Balkan societies into permanent international wards, excessively dependent on foreign funding and foreign troops. He said the Bush administration was determined to avoid a similar outcome in Afghanistan and Iraq.

In pursuit of this constricted vision of nation-building, the United States initially sought to minimize the size, geographical reach, and functions of the International Security Assistance Force in Afghanistan. Washington rejected Karzai's and the United Nations' pleas to deploy international peacekeepers outside Kabul. The administration opposed any role for NATO in Afghanistan and refused to allow American troops to perform any peacekeeping functions. Instead, it insisted that security for the Afghan population was to remain the regional warlords' responsibility until a new national army could be recruited, trained, and deployed. This process would take at least half a decade to complete and has in the event taken much longer.

In the first year following the Taliban's collapse, the United States committed approximately $500 million in reconstruction aid to Afghanistan, which works out to about $20 per Afghan. American aid to Afghanistan was only $700 million in 2003. That same year Congress authorized $18 billion for Iraq, a country smaller and less populous than Afghanistan and certainly less badly damaged. In 2004 Khalilzad succeeded in getting U.S. assistance raised to $2.2 billion, but in 2006, after he left Kabul, this figure was cut in half.

If there is a lesson to be drawn from the Afghan experiment in frugal nation-building, it is "low input, low output." When one applies low levels of military manpower and economic assistance to the tasks of post-conflict stabilization and reconstruction, one reaps low levels of security and economic growth.

Both the Afghan and Iraqi invasions proved that it is possible to substitute firepower for manpower and thus enable smaller, more agile forces to rapidly prevail over much larger, less-advanced adversaries. In this regard the Bush-Rumsfeld vision of military transformation proved quite apt. Subsequent experience has also shown, however, that in post-conflict stabilization and reconstruction operations, there is no substitute for "boots on the ground." Employing firepower as an alternative to manpower tempts spoiler elements to challenge the smaller force and results in greater casualties when they do, both for the occupying force and the occupied population, and thereby antagonizes the very people whose collaboration is essential to the operation's success.

By 2004, the administration began to boost its aid and military manning levels in Afghanistan. Rumsfeld withdrew his opposition to an expanded deployment of international peacekeepers and began recruiting allied contingents for this purpose. He also welcomed NATO involvement, urging the alliance to take over both the ISAF peacekeeping mission and the American-led counterinsurgency effort.

Meanwhile, nearly two vital years had been lost, years during which little progress had been made in extending effective governance to the countryside. As a result, by the time the threat of civil war reemerged, the population in the most vulnerable areas had little reason to risk their lives for a government that had shown no ability to protect them or to advance their material well-being.

One must look beyond Afghanistan, however, to understand why popular disappointment with the Karzai regime led to violent disaffection. Unlike the conflicts in Yugoslavia and Iraq, which arose principally from long-held antagonism among constituent nationalities, Afghanistan's long-running civil war has principally been the product of external intervention. In the 1980s, the Soviet Union and the United States used Afghanistan as a battleground in their global competition. In the 1990s, Pakistan, India, Russia, and Iran supported competing Afghan factions to protect and extend their influences in the region. In the current decade, the several insurgent groups that took up arms against the Karzai regime and its international backers arose in neighboring Pakistan.

The degree of official Pakistani complicity in the Taliban's resurgence is a matter of some controversy. In private, knowledgeable American, NATO, Afghan, and UN officials unanimously believe that the Pakistani Inter-Services Intelligence and Frontier Force have collaborated with the Taliban and other insurgent groups operating out of Pakistan's border regions. The Pakistani government at the highest levels, however, denies any official sanction for these activities, suggesting that, at most, former ISI members may be acting independently and against government policy.

Pakistan has both geopolitical and domestic incentives for allowing the Taliban and other radical groups to operate within its territory. Islamabad fears an Afghan state aligned with India and seeks to weaken those non-Pashtun factions that are susceptible to New Delhi's influence. Pakistan's Punjabi elites would also prefer to see Pashtun ambitions externalized—in the pursuit of power in Afghanistan—rather than turned inward toward the pursuit of greater autonomy or even independence for the Pashtun regions of Pakistan. If these considerations do not lead Pakistani officials to aid the Taliban insurgency, they at least diminish Pakistani incentives to help suppress it.

More recently reports have circulated about Iranian assistance to the Taliban. The volume of arms and money coming from Iran remains trivial when compared with that coming from Pakistan. Nevertheless, even the partial disaffection of Iran from the Bonn Conference coalition's support of Karzai is another blow to American efforts to stabilize Afghanistan. Further it is a reminder that such efforts cannot succeed without the neighboring states' support.

The decision to invade Iraq in 2003 diverted American manpower and money from Afghanistan. More important it distracted American attention from what is the true central front in any war on terror. That central front is neither in Iraq nor Afghanistan but in the border regions of Pakistan. Al Qaeda, after all, is now headquartered in Pakistan. The Taliban also operates out of Pakistan, as do several other terrorist groups seeking to expel international forces from Afghanistan. In the 1990s, Pakistan assisted the North Korean and Iranian nuclear programs. Potential terrorists in Western societies still travel to Pakistan—not Iraq, not Afghanistan—for inspiration, guidance, support, and direction.

Yet if Pakistan is the central front in the war on terror, it is not susceptible to an American military response. Pakistan is, after all, six times more populous than Iraq, and it has nuclear weapons. Other sources of influence will be required to have any success on this front. These sources should include diplomatic efforts to encourage both India and Pakistan to resolve their differences over Kashmir. That dispute, after all, is the root cause of radicalization in Pakistani society and the main reason the Pakistani government has aligned itself with terrorist groups in the past. American assistance programs should also address the economic and social needs of the Pashtun communities on both sides of the Afghan-Pakistani border. It will be of only limited utility to win the hearts and minds of Pashtuns living in Afghanistan if the still larger number of Pashtuns living in Pakistan remains hostile, ungoverned, and determined to expel foreign troops from Afghanistan. The United States should also work with both the Afghan and Pakistani governments to establish an agreed border regime and to legitimize the current frontier. Finally, the United States should continue to encourage Pakistan to move toward civilian rule. Fundamentalist parties have never fared well in elections there and fared particularly poorly in the 2008 election. It is ironic that until recently the United States has pushed hard for democratization in Iraq, Palestine, and Lebanon—three societies where free elections were likely to intensify sectarian conflict—but has remained largely passive regarding democracy in Pakistan, where the opposite effect is more likely.

Afghanistan has never been a self-sufficient state, and it probably never will be. It is simply too barren, inaccessible, and isolated to provide security and effective governance to its large and dispersed population. So unless Pakistan's government can be persuaded to abandon its reliance on extremist elements within its own society, halt its support for terrorism, provide its youth educational alternatives to fundamentalist madrassas, extend effective governance into its border provinces, and curtail the use of its territories by insurgent movements, there is little likelihood that Afghanistan will ever be capable of securing its own territory.

The situation is not hopeless, however. If the American and international commitment to Afghan reconstruction was late in coming, in 2008 the effort is more substantial. Washington has accepted the leadership burden it initially shirked. America's allies, and the international community in general, are much more heavily engaged in Afghanistan than in Iraq. Support among the Afghan people for this foreign presence and for the Karzai government remains high, although it is falling.

American and NATO military power may prevent the situation in Afghanistan from getting much worse, but only diplomacy will make it dramatically better. *After the Taliban* has illustrated how diplomacy once achieved a regional consensus to support peace in Afghanistan. That arrangement was allowed to unravel, however, as American attention shifted to Iraq, the situation of the porous Pakistani border regions was left unattended, and American relations with Iran deteriorated. Peace will not come to Afghanistan, or Iraq for that matter, until American military prowess is once again matched to an inclusive diplomatic strategy that has some prospect of gaining broad regional support.

INDEX

ABOUT THE AUTHOR

Ambassador James Dobbins has held State Department and White House posts under eight Presidents including Assistant Secretary of State for Europe, Special Assistant to President Clinton for the Western Hemisphere, Special Adviser to President Clinton and Secretary of State Albright for the Balkans, and Ambassador to the European Community under President George H. W. Bush. He handled a variety of crisis management assignments as the Clinton Administration's special envoy for Somalia, Haiti, Bosnia, and Kosovo, and was George W. Bush's first special envoy for Afghanistan.

In the wake of September 11, 2001, Dobbins was designated as the Bush Administration's representative to the Afghan opposition. Dobbins helped organize and then represented the United States at the Bonn Conference, where a new Afghan government was formed. On December 16, 2001, he raised the flag over the newly reopened U.S. Embassy in Kabul.

Dobbins currently directs the International Security and Defense Policy Center at the RAND Corporation, a nonprofit research institution. He is the principal author of *America's Role in Nation-Building: From Germany to Iraq*, *The UN's Role in Nation-Building: From the Congo to Iraq*, and *The Beginner's Guide to Nation-Building*.

Dobbins graduated from the Georgetown University School of Foreign Service, and served three years in the U.S. Navy. He is married to Toril Kleivdal, and has two sons.